the church weddings
HANDBOOK

The seven pastoral moments that matter

Insights from the Church of England's Weddings Project

GILLIAN OLIVER

THE CHURCH OF ENGLAND

wedding

faith · hope · love

CHURCH HOUSE PUBLISHING

Church House Publishing
Church House
Great Smith Street
London SW1P 3AZ

ISBN 978 0 7151 4278 5

Published 2012 by Church House Publishing
Copyright © The Archbishops' Council 2012

The opinions expressed in this book are those of the author and do not necessarily
reflect the official policy of the General Synod or The Archbishops' Council of the
Church of England.

Originated by Regent Typesetting, London
and printed in England by
CPI Group (UK) Ltd, Croydon, CR0 4YY

Contents

Weddings
Step-by-step

Register your couples at www.diary.yourchurchwedding.org/ for automatic reminders

For specialist invitational resources email weddings.project@churchofengland.org

Top tips and more at www.yourchurchwedding.org/project

FIRST CALL
Desktop guide
- A simple guide to the law to help you say 'yes!'

FIRST MEETING
Welcome pack
- A ribboned folder filled with advice and inspiration
- Refer them to their home church

HOW ARE YOU? HOW WERE WE?
Get in touch to ask for feedback from the couple.

1ST ANNIVERSARY
Anniversary Card
Most first anniversaries are on a Sunday. So why not invite them to come back again?

THE COUPLE'S BIG DAY
Congratulations card
To arrive when they get back from their honeymoon.

KEY

MARRYING CHURCH / HOME CHURCH

BANNS INVITATION
- Invitation to hear the banns reading and be prayed for. Both home and marrying churches send this.

'SPACE TO THINK'
- Invitation to think about the vows and the difference they make
- choose hymns and readings online at www.yourchurchwedding.org

the
weddings
project

www.yourchurchwedding.org

Preface

by the Archbishop of York

When the Archbishops' Council decided to commission the Weddings Project just five years ago this was one of the best decisions we ever made. At the time it was a shot in the dark. It could easily have turned out to deliver just one more Church report, confronting beleaguered clergy and congregations with yet another depressing set of statistics, with a few 'if only's tagged on to the conclusion. What we have here instead is dynamite.

Gillian Oliver and her team have been on tour conducting roadshows to share the findings of the project throughout the Dioceses of the Church of England. Clergy who have been to these have felt affirmed, challenged, informed, and inspired to go out and put these ideas into practice.

What is remarkable is that we should be so surprised and energized by something that, underneath, we all knew already. When I was a Vicar of Holy Trinity Tulse Hill we had plenty of enquiries about getting married – even in our Primary School Hall where we worshipped for ten years as we were fundraising to repair our Parish Church. Thank God we managed to restore Holy Trinity Church beyond its former glory. In those days couples came to see me in our home. There was no vestry! At Holy Trinity we did our best to make the process of preparing for weddings as personal as possible. I think we did quite well. But reading this book makes me think how we might have done things differently. I am sure many of you will come to the same conclusion.

This is a wake up call. People want to be married in church. They may be tongue tied, especially the men, when it comes to saying why, but beneath their search for 'the right venue' and whatever they may say about wanting a 'proper' wedding, there is a recognition that there is something important in a wedding that only begins to make sense when there is space for the sacred.

You don't have to be particularly religious to have a feel for the sacred. Plenty of people with little or no experience of church are awestruck at those all-or-nothing moments when a man and a woman pledge themselves to each other, 'for richer for poorer, in sickness and in health, till death us do part.' It is not only mothers and fathers of the bride who shed a tear when a couple take each other by the hand. But have we known what to do with this strong feeling of something special? The good news is that couples on the whole think we do a great job on the wedding day. Perhaps we have, in some small way, been helping them to open their eyes to the wonder of it all?

It may even be this same sense of awe that scares so many people off getting married – a commitment which they may not feel ready for, a burning of the boats which doesn't sit easily with our contemporary flair for keeping options open. What I am saying is that some people get married for the same reason that others choose not to – because it is such a patently obviously big thing. Perhaps by overfamiliarity those of us who take weddings may sometimes lose touch with just how big a thing this is?

When St Paul tells us that marriage can symbolize the relationship between Christ and his people, I don't think he is just using marriage as a sermon illustration. Marriage may, on the one hand, simply be a social institution defined by law as 'the union of one man and one woman, to the exclusion of all others', but it is much, much more. Accompanying a couple through the process of preparing for marriage, being alongside them as they marry to help them draw on the resources of faith, hope, and love which God has for them, and being there for them to support them in the future – as we promise in the service – all this is a wonderful privilege. 'A great mystery' as St Paul describes it.

At its most profound it is not we who define marriage, but marriage which shapes us. All of us owe our existence, one way or another, to the coming together of a man and a woman. Our very existence depends upon it. I don't mean merely our biological existence. It is our identity as members of the wider human family which is shaped by our childhood experience of a stable 'home'. Who we are is shaped not only by genetics, but by the nurture of those who care for us as children. What an awesome process all this is! No wonder some fight shy of the responsibilities that go with it and hesitate at the idea of getting married.

It will be a surprise to many, in an age where the meaning of the institution of marriage is widely debated, that there persists such wide recognition of these fundamental, spiritual values. I am thankful for the enormous encouragement the Weddings Project has given to clergy and parishes as they seek to respond warmly and imaginatively to those who come to us at these key moments in their lives.

When thinking about 'family values' it is easy for the church to get into a nostalgic and pessimistic frame of mind. We should remember that at the wedding at Cana, they were amazed that the best wine, so it seemed, had been kept until last. As we spend time in the presence of Jesus we can expect great things. And remember the Church does not belong to us. It belongs to Christ and all of us are his invited guests – his invited friends. This book makes me profoundly hopeful.

+Sentamu Ebor

Foreword

by The Venerable John Barton

I thought I was pretty good at weddings before I encountered the Weddings Project.

After all, I had always aimed to establish friendly relations with the couple as soon as I met them, tried to involve them in a serious but informal conversation about marriage and later worked with them to personalise the service. Although I could see that couples were a bit apprehensive and on their best behaviour from day one, I didn't realise the extent to which they approached their first encounter with a vicar – any vicar – with foreboding. The research which undergirds the Weddings Project has revealed that couples, and especially the men, fear they are on trial and unworthy of the Church's ministrations. Being friendly towards them is not enough. Something like absolution is needed from the outset, in the name of Jesus who specialised in attracting those people who regarded themselves as unsuitable candidates for his attention.

Like many clergy, I concealed my mild frustration when, in response to my question about the couples' reason for choosing church over Register Office, the man would be tongue-tied and look to his partner to answer. She would say something theologically inadequate like, 'it wouldn't feel the same' or stutter words about church being traditional. It did not seem a very substantial explanation. We now know that today's couples have plenty of choice when thinking about a venue for their marriage ceremony and when they come to us, they do so with serious intent, even though they do not have our language in which to express it. Brides-to-be tend to spend hours studying wedding magazines or the TV channels devoted to weddings, or trawling through the internet for ideas. These days more and more of them have come across the Weddings Project (www.yourchurchwedding.org) and have taken heart from its unreserved welcome before knocking on the vicarage door.

Another clerical myth has been dispelled by the Weddings Project research. The beauty of the church building is not the main motive for a church wedding. Once a religious ceremony has been decided upon, the prettiest church may be a factor, but that is not why 'church' is preferred to a picturesque castle or five-star hotel. The prime reason is an inner desire to do things properly and to take marriage seriously. It is for us to sense in this a genuine yearning for God's blessing, not least when enquirers feel themselves to be unqualified or unworthy to utter words like that. Marriage is an ordinance of Creation: it is God's gift to men and women and not the property of the Church. The couple are themselves the Ministers of the Sacrament. They marry each other. So it might be as well if we clergy were to bite our tongues when about to claim that we 'married' so-and-so. We didn't. They did!

The rehearsal provided an opportunity to get to know the main players, walk them through their parts and relieve their nerves with a bit of leg pulling. On the big day itself I would try to put everyone at ease, and then give the service 100%. The church was my home territory and I had developed ways of welcoming guests and explaining the difference between being a member of a congregation and just being an audience. It never occurred to me that I, too, was a guest in Christ's Church until Archbishop Sentamu made that clear in an interview for the Weddings Project. In one church in his diocese, four recently married couples have joined the congregation and three have been confirmed. Might that not be because the vicar made them feel as much at home in that church as she herself?

Having said goodbye to everyone after the service, I would walk back through the church, picking up the orders of service which had been left behind, and thinking that I would never see those people again. I was always touched when newly married couples sent me a postcard from honeymoon, but thought no more of it. The Weddings Project put paid to such complacency. Most would have appreciated a follow-up. I had no idea. Among the Project's system of resources is a method for achieving that without huge effort. In fact, the whole system has been devised and honed to show pre-churched people that we care for them and are honoured that they have chosen to be married in church. Secular wedding venues compete for their custom, with plush brochures and enticing stalls at wedding fairs, but have no further interest once the reception is over. Surely we, the servants of Christ who lavished his generosity on an unsuspecting couple at Cana, are not motivated by profit and can add value to all that.

With that in mind, what about fees? Church Councils in particular may say we do not charge enough. The basic fees (which are fixed by Parliament), before optional add-ons like music, bells and flowers, are a fraction of the sums spent on reception, photographs and carriages. The burden of maintaining church buildings falls on a few and it is tempting to feel a little resentful towards occasional users who have no idea of this responsibility. I have looked at a number of parish church websites which, perhaps for this reason, confuse legal fees with voluntary contributions. Additionally, a few websites have not been updated since the 2008 Marriage Measure became law and are now off-putting as well as inaccurate. Some others do not publish the vicar's contact details and seem to be written for insiders. Our communications, all of them well meant, may actually be conveying to readers the impression that God is out of reach and that the Church is a members-only institution.

I have visited hundreds of churches and talked with scores of Church Councils. Without exception, all asserted that they welcomed visitors. They meant it and in almost every case I could endorse that because I had been warmly received myself. I now know that the only person who has the authority to say whether a church is welcoming or forbidding is a newcomer. That certainly goes for Sunday services, but even more for the occasional offices attended by hundreds of thousands of visitors every year. Are there hidden trip-wires, unnecessary barriers, which we, without thinking, have put on their way to God?

To be a Christian means to encounter the risen Christ who was crucified, and to respond to the age-old invitation to follow him. That is a tough call: a real obstacle which we must not try to remove, for discipleship has a price attached. What we can do, though, is to ensure that we are not placing unnecessary stumbling blocks in the way of people before they have got that far.

Clergy reading this book will be surprised to discover how important they are. They may also be disconcerted to know that this may require them to devote to couples even more personal time and consideration than has been their practice. Yet here are people, usually not yet church members, who actually want our attention. How often does that happen in the course of a normal week?

The Church of England could be conducting more than double the number of weddings than the 22% we currently achieve. The Archbishops' Council saw in this an opportunity for church growth and set up the Weddings Project with that aim. If the reactions of clergy who have taken part in its presentations round the country is anything to go by, we are well on the way to our goal. Although I could have done with all this many years ago, it's thrilling to see this age-old Pastoral Office given new impetus. It really works.

John Barton

Introduction

When Jill and Kevin Peterson married in a Lutheran Church in Minnesota, some of the family couldn't make it to the wedding. So an uncle took a five-minute video and posted it on You Tube.

If you haven't seen it yet, search online for Jill and Kevin Wedding and press play.

It became a worldwide internet phenomenon. Friends sent it to friends who sent it to friends. After two years more than 70 million had watched it, and thousands posted goodwill messages or sent cash gifts to the couple's nominated charity.

What is going on when the world is magnetised by images of a bride arriving in a church on her wedding day?

––––––––––

On national radio a Church of England vicar condemns the spendthrift spirit of our times and its effect on the modern wedding. These are now, he says, 'too often a glitzy stage set, more concerned with the shoes, the flowers the napkin rings and performing to the cameras'.

Is a wedding nothing but a party for a culture consumed by celebrity, or a hallowed moment yearned for by a spiritually serious generation?

––––––––––

When Steve and Zoe dined one Valentine's night in Rugby, Steve had arranged for the waiter to bring a red rose with every course. When he proposed, Zoe agreed. They walked home as if on air. Suddenly, a church they had never noticed before seemed to loom up at the side of the road. Neither of them church goers, they went in to ask if they could marry there. They could. They did. And they never left.

What would it take for more people to discover church through their wedding and stick with it after the day?

———————

This book is about growing the Church, numerically and spiritually, through weddings.

It is a book for clergy. It contains insights for the people who support clergy in their weddings ministry, but it is mainly for clergy, or as we say in the Weddings Project, 'vicars'.

Why 'vicars'? You may not be a vicar. You may be a curate, a rector, a canon, NSM, LOM, SSM, or retired bishop. But if you are an ordained person spotted in or near a parish church then most people in England will call you a vicar. The Weddings Project has tried to see things from the public's point of view, and that has affected its public vocabulary. This is a book for vicars about growing the Church through weddings and it's based on the evidence that vicars really matter to the growth of the Church. If applied in seven simple ways, this evidence can increase the strength and depth of congregations everywhere.

Evidence-based growth

The Weddings Project is an idea of the Archbishops' Council, and it's an idea that grew out of the Church of England Marriage Measure of 2008. The Council has a set of objectives, the first of which is to grow the Church in depth and strength (see http://www.churchofengland.org/about-us/structure/ archbishopscouncil/objectives.aspx).

In 2008, when the General Synod initiated a new law to make it easier to marry in church, the Archbishops' Council came up with an idea to go with it. The idea was to discover what opportunities for church growth still lay in the age-old Anglican weddings ministry.

In the Weddings Project, the Church of England was doing something it had never done before. It was investing what amounted to a tiny percentage of income from a big ministry area in research and development for mission. From its investment the Archbishops' Council wanted to see a measurable difference, and it wanted facts to prove it. It wanted to know, for example, how much truth there is in the idea that people only choose church for the look of the building. It wanted to know why couples choose marriage, when living together is what they tend to do first. And the Council wanted to know what it would take to retain more people in the worshipping life of congregations. In other words, it wanted more of them to 'stick' after the wedding.

Over the course of the Weddings Project people have asked why we didn't branch out, for example into an investigation of other relationship choices, or take a particular interest in the marriage of people with a previous partner still living. Still others wished we had produced a critique of the liturgy or made more marriage-preparation resources. But the Archbishops' Council gave the team a focus on the changes the Marriage Measure would bring, and a deadline. If any ideas emerged which were intriguing but beyond scope, the team had to put them in a metaphorical fridge while they got on with the main thing. The measurable growth of the Church through weddings is what the work, and this book, is all about.

So the Weddings Project is a church growth project. And it is an evidence-based project.

In its quest for evidence, the Archbishops' team didn't go where the Church has gone before, like to books in libraries or to clergy conferences or to university professors. The Church of England decided to investigate matters by asking the public first. These were couples interviewed in their homes, or men recorded talking to their mates about love and marriage. They were brides at wedding shows and the general public through phone polling. They were not the only people who were quizzed about what they thought, but they were central. The Church went to them first.

Through diligent, public-focused enquiry the team demolished some big myths and uncovered good news. And when the Weddings Project team took the fruits of the work around the country, some people asked: 'Who are the theologians of marriage you have drawn from and where can we buy their books?'

The theologians of marriage are people like Sarah, Steve, Leanne, Dave and hundreds more. They don't normally go to church, but they went for a wedding, and they told us what they thought of it. What they said might surprise you and certainly gave something for the big thinkers in the Church to reflect on.

So this book does not bring you anecdote, supposition or hunch. When it comes to weddings, the Weddings Project has found out the facts.

Holy insights

As well as approaching the research task in a markedly different way from before, the Weddings Project team sought new insights from God in prayer. We were led to an icon from the Eastern tradition which shows the banqueting table in Cana and the wedding Jesus went to. Counter to the way things usually go with icons, Christ himself is not central. The couple is. Jesus is painted off to the edge, only recognisable because of the halo the artist has given him. He is near to the servants who are pouring out the miracle. His mother Mary leans against him, whispering in his ear (see http://parishable items.wordpress.com/category/salvation-history/wedding-of-cana/).

One or two around the table are startled by the quality of what's in their glass. The happy couple are delightedly oblivious to what is happening. Our Lord doesn't take any credit. He didn't take a bow. He didn't send a bill. Only the servants know what is really happening.

This idea, that weddings are a moment to put the couple centre stage and for those of us in the Church to take a lesser place at the edge of the action, led the team to York, and to Archbishop John Sentamu. In commissioning the Weddings team, he approved this way of thinking:

> I want the Weddings Project to be a way of saying to everybody: Come. You're welcome. Into God's church, where we are all guests, where we want everybody to come and find out about the love of God in Jesus Christ. That's what I did as a vicar, that's what I still continue to do. It is not my church, it's not vicar X's church, it's not parishioners X's or Y's church, but the church of Jesus Christ, in which we are his guests, he is the host. And he asks us by our worship, our prayer, our witness, to bring more and more friends to him.

This sort of idea has its foundation in the work of Bishop John V. Taylor. He wrote of baptism that the Church is guest – not host – at a sacrament instituted and graced by God. And this, of course, has particular resonance in marriage, as in Anglican theology the couple marry each other. *They themselves* are the ministers of the sacrament and the marriage is effected when they say their vows. It's their wedding. The Church brings its liturgy, its traditions and the legal direction and declarations. But the Church is not the host. Christ is the host.

So what does putting a couple centre stage mean? If it means putting their preferences ahead of our own, what are these preferences? And how can we say 'yes' to the things that unchurched people prefer while honouring all that's sacred, orderly and holy?

Their wedding, their church

In 1967 my mum was married, aged 23. In 1996 I was married, aged 27. Today's bride is 30, on average, and she's getting older (see http://www. telegraph.co.uk/news/uknews/8039651/Average-age-of-first-time-brides-is-now-30.html).

And the average age of a Church of England congregation is 62. It would be understandable if the culture and expectations of the gathered congregation are different from the bride and groom's. But if tensions arise, what should a church's response be? So the Archbishop's idea, built on the impulse of Bishop Taylor, became the Weddings Project's guiding star. When it came to a tie-breaker, we'd always ask this question:

'Whose church is it?'

Weddings are off

The context for all this is that the number of marriages is at an all-time low. Not since records began have there been so few weddings in the UK. The slide started, according to government records, in the seventies and for marriage it's been downhill ever since.

But weddings *in the Church of England* have fared much worse. For every three in the 70s, we only have one wedding now. When other venues became available for weddings in 1994, the downward trend continued. Altogether the Church has lost two thirds of its weddings while the overall slump in marriage has only been by about one third. So the Archbishops gave the Weddings Project three tasks:

- To **attract** more weddings in church.
- To **build** public awareness of the Church's enthusiasm for marriage through proactive media, wedding shows and online.
- And to **care** for couples and guests so well, more of them want to stick with church after the day.

The definition of folly

It is said that only a fool would keep on doing the same thing while expecting a different outcome. So driving up weddings and 'intention to stick' would necessarily require some parish-level changes in approach.

The Weddings Project worked in two Church of England areas to test new ideas in real churches. These were in the Diocese of Bradford and the Archdeaconry of Buckingham in Oxford Diocese. These are very different places in ministry context and wedding numbers, and they were home to the team while they researched and piloted and measured and reviewed. The result was a simple system of resources for churches everywhere to make life easier while serving couples better.

If you're in one of 33 partner dioceses you can use the materials already. If you're not sure whether your diocese is a partner or not, check www. yourchurchwedding.org/project

Motivation

Some people say the Archbishops must be desperate to go to all this trouble. It was a question that the Project's researchers kept asking us: What is a church's ultimate motivation? It's clear why fizzy drinks companies want to sell measurably more drinks. But why would vicars want to do more weddings? And of course, working with clergy in Bradford and Oxford, and meeting clergy all over the country, it is clear that life is busy enough. What would make vicars block out two days of their time to listen to a team from London sent from the Archbishops to ask them to do more weddings?

Having spanned the country and offered the findings to 3,500 vicars, mainly those who do the most weddings, I think I have seen what it is. It's a priestly trait. You can find shades of it in the book of Hosea and the Song of Songs. It's a quality of acutely gentle but persistent yearning for people who are distant from God. It's like God's *concern* for a foreign city, described in the book of Jonah. It's not bulldozing and it's not threatening. It's a wholesome desire to see the best brought out in the people that God made. It's the most winsome thing about the vicars of England. They are 'people' people. They came into ministry to sit on sofas with marrying couples, and pay them the compliment of really listening. If they had ever got diverted from that main thing, if they had ever delegated it, Sarah, Steve, Leanne and Dave were recalling them to it.

Whose church is it? Not ours.

So what is our right motivation? How do we feel about the people who, for a shimmering instant, cross our path? Not a desperation which is without hope, but the sort that longs, with Christ, to grow his Church.

Secular research

Our partners throughout this journey of discovery were commercial – not academic – researchers. They are the sort who usually find things out for governments and industry. They kept the project team honest about what it was finding out. And they kept the findings robust, since the Church was never seen to be the one asking the questions. The Project's lead researcher, Tamar Kasriel, formerly of the Henley Centre and now of Futureal, is more used to working with the Cabinet Office and Coca Cola. So what was it like to work with the Church of England? She says:

> 'It's been a really fascinating project: it's quite an unusual organisation. But I think we saw you as something of a dream client. Nothing is done thoughtlessly, there's nothing haphazard about what you ask and what you want to find out. What marks you out as well is a genuine interest in getting to the answer – there's a genuine curiosity there. And nothing we found out was wasted. It's quite rewarding as a researcher to know what you are discovering is going to be used and not going to sit in a cupboard somewhere.'

The findings, hewn from two focused geographical areas, north and south, affluent and austere, have applicability across the whole Church of England and now every diocese has had a chance to receive them. You may be reading this because you were at a Weddings Project presentation in the 75% of dioceses in which the bishop invited us to work. But if you missed it, this book is also for you. It's designed to record what the Weddings Project learned so that none of it need go to waste, and every church in England can know its secrets.

Moment One:
The First Call

A church wedding typically starts some 18 months before the big day itself, when a couple gets in touch about their good news. So let's shine a light on this first moment of their church wedding experience. The evidence is that this is the most crucial moment for a church to get right, and identifies the best person to be 'front of house' in any church at this moment. Who it is could surprise you.

- **Who's in touch first, and how do they feel?**

- **How did they know about the church and who to contact?**

- **What one thing means they might never get in touch?**

- **How serious are couples about marriage?**

- **How serious are they about God ?**

- **What does the law require of churches?**

It all begins when the phone first rings. Or does it? In research in Bradford and Oxford two thirds of couples contacted the church in the first instance by phone. We do realise that this is changing very fast, and we'll get to the growing potential of e-contact soon. However, one thing does not change much at all, and that is who makes first contact with the church. It's the bride. According to our research in two dioceses, nearly 80% of first contacts involve the bride, either on her own (in more than half the cases) or together with her fiancé. It is less common to be approached by the groom alone (12%), a parent (8%) or grandparent (1%).

This evidence caused the Weddings Project to pay particular attention to the bride at these opening moments of the church wedding journey. It's one reason we hired women writers and designers to put together the words and images that form the materials we offer to couples through churches. We are a female-led project, and we are communicating mostly, and particularly at first, with women. What the Project found out about men comes into sharper focus a little later in the church wedding journey.

But when the phone first rings it will usually be the bride on the other end. So, how is she feeling when she makes that call? And first of all, what is she thinking about marriage?

England is serious

Latest government research indicates that about 80% of people who marry have lived together first. This often gives rise to much chatter predicting the end of the road for such an 'anachronistic rite'. In churches, and outside them, the accusation is sometimes heard that couples today cannot be serious about marriage, since it will not change much in their lives. When they eventually choose to get married, it must be because they love to party.

Jesus said that giving and being given in marriage will go on enthusiastically right to the end, meanwhile trends come and go. For a couple of decades it was the done thing for women to keep their maiden name when they married. Big stars like Victoria Beckham and Cheryl Cole changed all that when they chose to take their husband's name and this is now the more usual thing among today's brides.

To find out the broad themes among people considering marriage today, researchers took video cameras into couples' homes and asked them what they really thought and felt. These were independent research teams and there was not a dog collar in sight when this research work was done. That's how we met Dave and his partner from the Midlands. They own a home together and they live in it together. They have plans to extend it, but something is missing. What is it? Dave's partner explains:

> 'I'm a lot more old fashioned where it's concerned. It's not like I think 'Oh it's terrible that we live together', it's not that. I just want to be your wife [laughs] … whereas Dave's not really bothered. It's like the final show of your commitment. Dave says we will do it, maybe when the extension's finished. Well if we wait till the extension's finished we'll never do it.'

You really have to watch this exchange to feel Dave's discomfort. He appears to want to shuffle right off the end of his sofa. In fact some of us wondered if his partner had ever got round to saying these things before a research team and film crew turned up in their sitting room. Some of us in the team found it moving, even heartbreaking. But we were all listening to the laughter that accompanied the revelation.

In the Weddings Project we have found that laughter and seriousness go together a lot. We have banks of films of people laughing when they get to the point of expressing something serious, about God or each other. Anthropologist Kate Fox in *Watching the English* writes of a nation with an 'oh come off it' impulse that is uncomfortable with expressions of earnestness. That discomfort can find a release in laughter. And the evidence suggests that when ministering to a generation which is wordless when serious, the pastoral art is to listen for the yearning under the laugh.

The phrase Dave's partner used, 'the final show of your commitment', chimes with others used by many couples in the research. Some spoke of marriage as 'the last piece in the jigsaw', 'the final frontier', 'the gold standard'. And listening to this we began to learn that marriage occupies an entirely different place in the hearts and minds of contemporary culture. For my parents, my grandparents and generations before them marriage has been the gateway to adult life. Not any more.

So this is a view of marriage unique to this generation. Couples today see marriage as more like a *crown* on a relationship which has proved itself to be trustworthy and true, and not the threshold of adulthood, as it once was.

It comes later in life, at an average age of 30, and rising. A question our researchers asked in a nationwide survey of the general population bears this out. They asked: 'Which event best indicates to you and to other people that you are committed to each other for life?'

Almost no one thought that buying a car together expressed this very well, and other low-ranking options were making a will together, being engaged or 'just knowing you were right for each other'. Closer to top of the pops, but not there yet, were moving in together (18%) and having children together (21%). But the absolute winner – nothing scored anything like as high – was getting married (42%). There is still nothing beyond marriage to show each other and the world that you are committed to each other for life.

Exclusive romantic relationship, as proclaimed in marriage, carries a high value. The evidence suggests there's nothing higher. Perhaps it is valued more highly by this generation, for whom there is no social stigma in not marrying, because it is a positive choice, from a range of others, made freely, without strong social constraints.

So marriage may have a higher value in the mind of the bridal generation, but it shows its results, its consequences, less conspicuously. It is less likely than in the past to be accompanied by a new address, new habits or a van full of G-Plan furniture. Marriage today is a crowning glory on a love well lived and this is why there is this desire for a wedding to be perfect. If it's a crown, it's a reward, it's a culmination, a haven, a longed-for destination. It's less likely to be fully expressed with paper plates and cheap plonk. All the lavish feasting that can accompany a modern wedding is part of the same idea. Not every couple wants to spend a fortune, and as Christian people we might prefer not to either, but spending and lavishness is a corollary to this fact:

A perfect crown is what they are yearning for, when they yearn for marriage.

This seriousness about marriage has implications for the wedding day itself and the way in which we in the Church prepare couples for it. When people choose to marry, marriage is what they want, and nothing else gets near to what they want to say through it. They want to proclaim their seriousness about each other for the rest of their lives. Meanwhile, it's true that numbers of marriages, as a proportion of the population, continue to decline. It has never been so little undertaken since records began. But researchers of all kinds agree that delay, not necessarily disinclination, is one big reason why numbers are falling.

So this is what one thirty-year-old bride is thinking about marriage when she picks up the phone to you. No matter what her living arrangements are, she is super serious about marriage. However, it's true that her idea of marriage is very likely to be categorically different from yours, and from all the generations of vicars before you.

A church wedding

Why does she want church for a wedding? She might say she would like to 'book the church' and that turn of phrase may irritate you. She may explain that she was just driving by one weekend and picked it because of its beauty. She may say that to compliment you. She doesn't know it might not. But it stands to reason, doesn't it, that the beauty of the building is what people want when they want a church wedding? Prettier churches do most weddings, so more brides must want a beautiful backdrop than want God.

We met vicars on our tour of England who really struggled with what I'm about to tell you. And we met vicars who always knew the truth of it, but who were glad to discover why they know what they know. This is what the Weddings Project found out:

Most people think a church wedding 'feels more proper'.

That's the finding of a poll of the general population by a national secular research agency. 53% of the population agreed with the statement, 'Church weddings feel more proper.' You are more likely to agree with this statement if you are a younger person and if you are a male person. So it is not a phenomenon that is due to die out, it is a research finding that is 'future-proof'. You may not think it is a sky-high figure but it is, compared to the number of weddings we're doing. We are not marrying 53% of the marrying population in the Church of England. We are only marrying 22% (all churches together account for about 33% of all weddings). So the Church of England could easily conduct double the number of weddings by just marrying the people who thought that church was the right place for it, never mind persuading anyone else about it.

A 'proper' wedding

This word 'proper' has become a key for the Weddings Project and it is packed with meaning and application. To help us understand it, we spoke to academics including sociologists of religion. What they told us lay behind the word 'proper' gave us so much hope for the spiritual seriousness of England that we weren't sure whether to believe them. So in a more focused survey of 822 people marrying in Bradford and the Buckingham Archdeaconry of Oxford our research team probed more deeply. They asked them what *the main reason* was for choosing church for their wedding. Not *a* reason, but *the* reason. They asked people in groups, at three points along the journey:

- at the moment of first contact (before they were married but when they were first in touch with the church)

- around the time of the ceremony

- and a year later.

One option researchers gave as the main reason for marrying in church was this: 'The main reason for choosing church for me personally was the appearance of the church or chapel.' And here's what they found: before the day only 4% said the main reason they chose church was because of its appearance. Of those questioned around the time of their wedding, only 1% said that was the main reason. And a year after the day, not a single person questioned could say that the look of church was the standout reason they chose it for their wedding.

On the other hand, a number of other reasons were advanced by more than 80% of the people questioned as *the main reason* for choosing church over any other venue. And they were all God reasons. They were things like this: 'We wanted to make our vows before God'; 'We wanted to ask for his blessing'; 'We wanted a spiritual side to our wedding'; 'We wanted the sacred ambience of the church'; 'It was something to do with my family's faith or mine' (or my partner's faith or mine); 'We wanted a proper wedding'; 'We wanted a traditional wedding.'

Our researchers found that for about two thirds of couples the appearance of the building is a reason to choose *a particular church over another*. But when it comes to choosing to be married in church at all, it hardly figures. Only one in a hundred would say they had originally chosen church for what meets the eye.

So this word 'proper' comes to the Church from a wordless world, tied up in all these other high-scoring phrases about God and his felt presence. It's a word more commonly used by couples in the south of England, and it's a counterpart to 'traditional' which is used more in the north. It's not a word that necessarily describes things you can see. It's a word about story, ceremony, depth, rightness, seriousness, appropriateness, gravity and dignity. All words which align with what God brings to a marriage service.

To find out a little more about what 'proper' feels like, here's how one mother of the bride put it when she walked into a church in Worcestershire with her daughter Nicky. What she said was filmed by the BBC for their hit show *Don't Tell The Bride*. 'For me, it's not about your wedding, this place', Nicky's mum said. 'It's the essence of the place, the feel of the wood, it's just a calmness that descends. The true essence of marriage is a promise in the eyes of God to one another. It's got to be, hasn't it? It's got to be in a church.'

Lost in translation

Women are more likely to talk about spirituality by talking about how they feel. I don't know how many people who come to church where you are say they did so because of the 'feel of the wood'. But most of us can relate to that phrase of Nicky's mum's: the calm that descends, the wonder of promise-making in the sight of God. Because we live in a culture that is losing the language of orthodox Christian belief, other words are being used instead, foundational words about yearning, experience and value. There is a good chance we might not recognise them as God words when we first hear them. These days, some things are lost in translation, and that might mean the moment of seriousness is shrouded with laughter, or it might mean that the words people use can leave us sensing they are not serious, when in fact they are.

Sarah, a beautician from the north of England, is marrying in church in the village where she grew up. She hasn't been back since she was in the Brownies. So why does she want to marry there? 'We've always wanted to get married in church, because it's traditional and it means more than just a hotel room. You've got God's blessing if you like', and she starts to laugh. Laughing in the sense of 'me, talk about God's blessing? How ridiculous does that sound?'

A bride from Oxfordshire spoke to our researchers wistfully about this failure to communicate with the vicar on the first meeting. 'I think he just thought I was some girl that wanted a big white wedding, rather than the fact that it had any sentimental value to it.' Sentimental value? You or I may be tempted to hear the word 'sentiment' over the word 'value', but this bride was expressing her seriousness in the only words she had.

So let's get back to our bride on the other end of your phone. We have established that she is serious about marriage. Even though to her it might mean something different from what it means to you, and sits later in life, she is no less serious about it. She doesn't have to get married, after all. What can we conclude then about why she is ringing you – why she wants to marry in church? Well, she doesn't have to choose church. If she just wants a beautiful building there are plenty of those available on the secular wedding scene. So your bride wants to marry in church because she wants God there. And of course that is a very promising place to begin.

Seriousness meets a block

So with all this seriousness in England today, yearning for marriage and desire for God's blessing, it must be the simplest thing in the world for a bride to pick up the phone to you and ask if you would conduct their wedding for them. Yes?

No.

Researchers discovered that this seriousness meets a big block somewhere. What they found is that brides are unlikely to get to the point of picking up the phone in the first place. So big are the obstacles in their own mind, they are more likely to give up altogether without even trying and go somewhere else instead.

We have to take you to one sofa in England, and to one bride and groom talking about their 'yes' and 'no' to choosing a church wedding. On the face of it they should be untroubled. They are connected under the law because the bride's parents married in the church and so can they. The legal right extends now to them just as if they were resident in the parish. So what's the problem then? The bride spells out the dilemma:

> 'Yeah, I've always thought I'd get married in a church, but I do feel a bit *hypocritical* because I'm *not particularly religious*. My parents got married in the same church we're getting married in, which is nice for me but it doesn't sit very easily for me. I think if we both felt the same way as I do then I'd feel very unhappy about getting married in church, which is such a shame because I do want to get married in church … but for the wrong reasons probably.'

It's impossible to overstate how high the barrier can be in the couple's own minds because of their felt 'hypocrisy'. Now of course, into this lack of qualification and fear of rejection the Church of England has good news to bring. Because we are the Church of England the good news, made even better by the Marriage Measure of 2008, is that we marry people, and so there are churches in England for people to marry in. They do not have to be churchgoers, nor baptised, nor anything else.

The feeling among the marrying generation that they are being hypocritical is the number one myth that the Church of England has to explode. Because of this fact, it works less and less well if we in the Church of England just wait for brides to come and knock on the door. The Weddings Project realised that we had to get to couples while they were still yes-ing and no-ing on their sofas. That's why the website, www.yourchurchwedding.org is listed number one on Google on a search for church weddings, and why the national church is supporting the mushrooming provision of Church stands at wedding shows. It's all part of a plan to reach a 'hypocritical' generation with the good news of unqualified acceptance.

Back to your bride at the end of the phone. How is she? She is serious about marriage and God. But she is inexpert and wordless, feeling hypocritical, disqualified and uneasy. The obstacles she has overcome to pick up the phone and wait until you answer it are great. She is a heroine, a person of extreme courage. And she is about to be the recipient of great news.

The spirit of Marriage Law

You may think you are well versed on the law of England as far as eligibility for a church wedding goes, and the right way to set fees and charges. Even so, you may feel surprised at some of what follows, you may even feel repentant. If you do not feel repentant then you may be required to repent. But if you *are* well versed in these matters, then what follows will at least reassure you.

The Weddings Project uncovered that even the most seasoned parish priest can be holding on to errors passed down over the years. Some church people can get confused about exactly what is determined by statute and what by local practice. And marriage law does sometimes change. Indeed, it has just undergone something of a revolution. And the law on fees has been under review too. Add to this the fact that most people get engaged at New Year or on Valentine's Day. Vicars told us that these seasons are more likely to be times when they may not have done a wedding for a while. So, it's easy to get rusty. On such occasions, it's always good to know where to start. Let's start with the spirit of the law:

The Church of England is not a religious club for members. Its sacraments and services are for all the people of England.

In the case of a wedding you will know that this means that any engaged person who has not been married before has a legal right to marry in the church of the parish in which they live. Apart from a couple of very rare exceptions, this basic right is absolute. It is not conditional on their being baptised, on their churchgoing prowess or even on their readiness to say that they are Christian. As long as they are content to make the promises contained in the marriage service and they haven't already made them to someone else, if they are a parishioner of yours then you are obliged to welcome their wedding.

Now of course, this might mean that people will be marrying in your church while at the same time believing all sorts of mixed up things about Jesus and his divinity, reincarnation, angels, yoga and Sunday shopping. It doesn't matter. In these matters the law speaks of a Church of England which is big on grace. Even if one or both parties is divorced with a previous partner still living, the General Synod accepts their marriage in church at the vicar's discretion and has done so since 2002. Clergy make that call in the light of House of Bishops' advice. Couples with divorce in their story do sometimes write to the Church of England via the website www.yourchurchwedding. org and ask for a list of churches in their area that will marry divorcees. We always reply that each couple's story is different and your vicar will want to talk to you about yours. Many clergy speak of the particular privilege of ministry with couples who have known the pain of divorce and want God to help them start again.

So there is a fundamental right to a church wedding. It may be not well known in England today, but that does not take away from the truth of it. It means that, churchgoer or not, your local church is open to you, and you are welcome to this sacrament without promise of improvement. It is an impulse very close to a statement attributed to Archbishop William Temple, that the Church of England is the organisation that exists for people not its members.

The Weddings Project's research did find new evidence about couples' seriousness about God. This is true. However, being serious about God is not a legal requirement, and you cannot legally put anything in the way of couples except the demands of the law.

The Marriage Measure

Following a period of dramatic and sustained social mobility in England, Church leaders began to wonder if the law was actually causing them to turn away more people than they were marrying. People who moved away from a parish were instantly barred from marrying there. People whose parents or grandparents were married in a church had no consequent right to celebrate their wedding there too. It became evident that the law was too restrictive, and so the Church took the initiative to reform it.

In doing so it extended the basic parishioner's right in an amendment the like of which has not been seen since marriage law itself was first framed. This added seven new ways to marry in a church where you do not live. These are set out in full at *Find a Church* at www.yourchurchwedding.org.

What it means is that there is no distinction in law between an engaged person resident in your parish and one who has a connection with it under the Church of England Marriage Measure of 2008. So it is against the law for a church to differentiate between the two in any way. A church may not charge these two any differently. It cannot refuse either of them their wedding because there is no vicar there to do it, or if the vicar is disinclined. This is not a matter of good practice, but the law. Even if there isn't a connection in law, a couple can still make one by coming to the church for six months (once a month will do). After that, a new provision of the Marriage Measure means they are connected to the church without needing to be entered on the Electoral Roll. You and they can then set the date. Or they may apply for a Special Licence, or you may recommend that they are married by Superintendent Registrar's Licence. And even if there is absolutely no way legally to marry a couple in your church, you can still refer them to a church where they can. You could say that even if you have to say 'no' to a wedding in a particular church, you can still say 'yes' on behalf of the wider Church of England.

In a more recent and lesser-known amendment to the Marriage Measure, if a person has a connection to one church in a benefice, the bishop can extend that to every benefice church. If you're not sure whether your bishop has effected this direction in your diocese please check with your registrar. So these are the new rights. Not ecclesiastical guidelines, but law as set down by statute and unchangeable unless by Act of Parliament.

A simple guide to the law

The Weddings Project spoke to 174 clergy in Bradford and Oxford about marriage law, and found some confused. Vicars wanted 'a bullet point guide, written in Coronation Street language', and not another book or pamphlet that could quickly lose itself in the growing pile of papers in the study. They wanted a guide that was legally correct but not written by lawyers. So we have produced a simple guide to the law to keep by the phone to be an *aide-mémoire* when brides first call. It has become one of the Project's most popular resources. If you weren't at one of the presentations around the country you will have missed the handy self-assembly cardboard version, but you can download the same information at www.yourchurchwedding.org/project

Qualifying: a note

It was a bad day for the Weddings Project when the General Synod alighted on the word 'qualifying' to go with the word 'connection' to describe the seven new ways it wanted to welcome more weddings. That's because all words carry a charge, and in the case of qualifying it's not a positive one. Because we know how unhelpfully the word qualifying compounds the sense of *disqualification* in couples, you won't find us using it in any of our online resources or paper materials. We use the term *special connection* instead. Or just *connection* will do. You might want to do the same.

Foreign nationals

Of course social mobility is a not just a national phenomenon, it's global. But recent media coverage about sham marriages has given rise to anxiety among churches receiving enquiries from non-British nationals. However, the law still holds; the Church of England has a duty to marry people who are resident in England and eligible to do so, wherever they are from. All clergy are naturally keen to ensure that all Christian marriages be honestly undertaken and legally binding, and so special diligence in these cases is appropriate.

So how do you welcome a couple in a way that is true to the spirit of the law, while ensuring you also keep to the letter of it?

If one or both parties is a foreign national, and by foreign is meant from outside the European Economic Area, your Diocesan Registrar will give you specialist help and advice so that all that is lawful is attended to. These couples need to apply for a Common Licence to ensure that the marriage is recognised in their home country. One or two dioceses have, at time of writing, initiated their own provisions in these cases, so it's good to be clear about what's current where you are. The Church of England website always carries the latest explanation and direction from the House of Bishops.

The Weddings Project team met 3,500 vicars in its training tour of England, and the presentation team was peppered with vicars on secondment from active parish ministry. It does seem that if you're the sort of vicar who conducts many weddings, it happens, very infrequently, that when a couple gets in touch there's something about their story that doesn't feel right to you. In these cases, trust your instinct and call your friendly registrar. She or he is retained by your diocese to support you in your ministry and give you all the advice you need.

The Law on fees and charging for a wedding

So, we *must* marry couples if one of them has a connection with the church in law, or is resident in the parish. And we *may* marry them again even if they have been married before, as long as one of them has one of these connections. So that's the law and here is the news. A wedding, according to the wedding industry, costs an average £20,000. How are we to make sense of what we charge for weddings in the light of that, some would say, eye-watering figure?

Of course we churchgoers love our churches and want Christian ministry to continue there, but they are not our own enterprises. We cannot raise funds from them unlawfully, nor would we want to treat people unjustly in the pursuit of balanced books. The spirit of the law sets the scene for us.

We have the privilege of conducting weddings because of a calling not initiated by us, in a building provided for the purpose and because the Church of England is as it is – by law established. The law on fees is as simple as 1,2,3. It is set out for couples at www.yourchurchwedding.org where the *Cost of a Wedding* pages are among the most popular on the site.

Here are the three things every vicar and parish church needs to know (that includes cathedrals which are also parish churches). You will find this set out for clergy and churches in *The Reasonable and Clear Guide to Charging for a Wedding* at www.yourchurchwedding.org/project

1: Fees

Everyone who is entitled to marry in a church can do so for the statutory fee and no more.

The statutory fee covers all that is legally required to marry in church. It covers use of the building, lighting, ministry time, writing out the certificate and all related administration. You may believe the statutory fee to be inadequate to cover the costs of a church wedding, or you may believe it to be generous. Your views may interest your General Synod representative, but they are not at all relevant in law.

2: Charges

Any charge above the statutory fee is an optional extra.

Extras, over and above the basic legal service, can include things like bells and choir, flowers, organ music, heating, a verger and set-piece preparation events. Couples are not obliged to choose any of these things, but if they choose them then they will pay extra for them.

3: Gifts

Donations must be freely given.

On top of 1 and 2, couples may wish to give a gift. You can lawfully request a donation but you may not lawfully make the wedding conditional on it. Donations (but not fees or charges) can be gift aided.

It's as simple as that.

Very occasionally a church is surprised to find that it is unlawful to add a charge for use of the building. It's because the law gives a person who is eligible the right to use the building. No one then can lawfully interfere with that right by imposing charges on them. Likewise, charges for preparation, in the way the church likes to offer it, may not be lawfully imposed on the couple as a condition of their wedding. Only if a couple opts for this sort of preparation will they need to pay extra for it. The ministry costs of preparing a couple for their wedding are already included in the basic fee, since it is a basic duty of the priest to provide it.

The Law on deposits

Since payment of the statutory fee is a payment for a legal service, you cannot lawfully insist on it until the legal service has been delivered. However, if it suits the couple to give some part payment before their wedding, you may receive it – as long as it is fully returnable. If the wedding does not go ahead for whatever reason, and you have not called banns, you cannot lawfully retain any part of the statutory fee. If you have called banns, you can legitimately retain just that part of the fee.

If a couple has a question about how their marrying church is charging them, they can contact the Weddings Team via the website www.yourchurch wedding.org and we will look into it on their behalf. But it's very rare for us to hear from couples who have had each element explained in a pastorally warm encounter, and their choices clearly itemised from the outset.

At its heart the law speaks of a Church which is not ours, except that we can share it. It's not ours to profit from, nor to decline the marriage of anyone who is eligible. Because the Church of England is there for England, we are obliged to welcome weddings, and to set fees and charges according to the law.

Fear

So girls are in the lead when it comes to a wedding. But we did find out something crucial about what *men* think and feel at these opening moments of the church wedding journey. Women may feel the same, but men articulate this more powerfully. It was a crucial discovery because it gave a clue as to who, in the best of all worlds, should be the person 'front of house' for the church when a couple first gets in touch.

But first, a health warning about how to do proper research with men when it comes to issues of love and marriage: men prefer to leave the talking to the woman. If she is in the same room as him, you may never hear from him at all.

The only way you can really find out what men think, researchers advised, is to put them in a room with other men, get them talking together and set the cameras rolling. So that's what we did, and that's how we found one burly young man, the sort you would want on your side if you were caught up in a nasty brawl, telling the story of his first meeting with the vicar.

> 'I was more nervous that day than on my wedding day. I had a cup of tea in my hand and it was shaking, because you're in a place of worship where you can't swear, you can't do this or that. And you're being asked what your thoughts are and how many times you go to church. And I say 'oh, three times a month at least'. And I'm blatantly lying, and I feel really bad about it, but it's either that, or miss out on the most important day of our lives.'

This man was seriously scared. This fear factor in men was something we also spotted in a sequence on the BBC's *Don't Tell the Bride,* a programme in which the groom organises the wedding with little time, money, and no input from his bride. In it, another strapping man drives to his parish church to ask the vicar if a wedding there would be possible. He comes out of the meeting thumping his chest with his fist, and turning to his friend, says, 'That was the hardest thing I think I've ever done. My heart's pounding.'

These little exchanges are part of a wider research case which proves with very little doubt that meeting a vicar is a scary business. Do you sense fear in the couples you meet, when there's nothing at all to be scared of? One vicar at a Weddings Project event went straight on to an appointment at the hairdresser, and got talking about this there. The hairdresser put down her scissors and began to cry. 'I've been wanting to talk to you about this for so long … I want to marry in church but I've been afraid to ask. You see, my fiancé is black, and I didn't know if you would allow that.'

The fact of having children already is a more common reason why couples fear their church will refuse to marry them. Research in two dioceses revealed that one in five couples already has children, either through their relationship or a previous one. One vicar told of how a groom came to him on the morning of the wedding to tell him about a child by a previous partner. The vicar was sad that the young man didn't feel able to mention this sooner, but perhaps the groom had decided to wait for the point at which it was too late for the vicar to take his wedding away. Because of the potential for couples with children to 'self-disqualify', the Weddings Project worked with the Liturgical Commission to issue guidelines for combining a marriage service with a thanksgiving for the birth of a child or baptism. It's a way of offering 'a fresh start for the whole family', as the Bishop of Wakefield explained in a wide range of supporting media interviews.

Fear is a fact. At the end of one of our two-day presentations one vicar wrote in feedback, 'I had a very helpful conversation with one of our couples last night as a direct result of thinking that the groom might be fearful. That in itself was worth two days of my time.'

Other clergy have shared how couples might come across as a bit overconfident in conversation. They recognise, in the light of this research, that this itself might be the bluff and bluster of a fearful mindset. Fear does have its roots in the things we've already set out. People feel like hypocrites. They try to tell us they are serious but they do not speak our language. The combination of these things really can induce fear, and fear can make a person lie.

So a young man who doesn't go to church three times a month but feels he needs to tell the vicar he does, is blatantly lying by his own admission. And of course there's a strong chance that the vicar, who is no fool, is thinking, 'This person is blatantly lying to me.' What happens next? Hypocrisy in couples, giving way first to fear, then to dishonesty, can foster disdain in our churches. If this goes unchecked, it reinforces a couple's sense of hypocrisy instead of absolving it.

So, here is the picture that's emerging. A bride picks up the phone to a Church of England where weddings have been on the slide for forty years. She need not get married, and she need not get married in church. That she has decided to do both reveals her seriousness about both. However, she doesn't know the right words to use. She wishes she did. She feels like a hypocrite, she feels afraid. Out of a desire to have the most important day of her life she may lie about her religious observance. And her church may misunderstand what is really in her heart.

One person makes the difference

But into this complicated picture steps one person who can cut through all these difficulties better than anyone else in your church. The Weddings Project team did not expect to find this truth shining out from the research. But we did find it and so we have to tell you. This special someone may not be the person placed 'front of house' in the church where you are. But according to the Weddings Project's research, this particular person should be positioned at the point where the unchurched public comes through the door. If this person was waiting at the door to meet the newcomer, research indicates that more people would experience God's own welcome when they came to ask about a wedding. And more people would stick with church after the big day. Who is it?

I can't give you the answer as well as a newly wed couple from Bradford did. They put it this way in a research interview recorded on video:

> 'He's a vicar. He's a stereotypical vicar. He's always smiling. You want to call him 'father', like Christians do. But he's just a really nice guy. You feel like you could go to him and talk to him about anything, and that, I suppose, is what a vicar is there for.'

Why did our researchers find that a good experience of the vicar makes the biggest difference? Why is it the vicar that couples are secretly after?

Consider what we have already discovered, that unchurched couples are feeling hypocritical when they approach the church for a wedding. They do not feel, in their own words, 'particularly religious'. To them, the vicar is the person who is most clearly identified as *the chief God person* in the church. They believe the vicar will decide whether or not they are appropriate people to marry in church. When that person smiles at them and remembers things about them, and keeps in touch a little, it carries a peculiarly positive charge. That the vicar is a sinner with holiness conferred on them like any one else is neither here nor there. We are not considering how the world looks to us, even if we are right. We're choosing to see it the way a newcomer sees it, in the hope of serving them better.

The ordained just appear differently to the public. They communicate something about God and something about authority. The prospect of meeting such a person is scary if you regard yourself as the polar opposite. And people who feel they have no authority or language to talk about God, might think, 'Oh well I'm not in his or her club and I doubt they'll be interested in me.' But if they get that person's welcome up front and early in the church wedding process they are amazed, and very pleasantly surprised. They thought they were the B team and they got the A team. It's the sort of experience that causes a person to think: 'Who, me? Who am I that I should be taken this seriously?' And that, at least the way I understand it, is what it is like to discover grace.

When a vicar take a couple's seriousness seriously, it's a bit like an experience of grace – God's welcome for them. Indeed, what the Weddings Project found out about this particular pastoral office is this. Welcoming newcomers who are not churched is something the vicar can do more meaningfully and with more impact than a lay person. This is only because of how the ordained are commonly perceived by most people today. By the same token, our research found that when they get a lay person looking after them for too long it may feel to them as if they are being kept away from meeting the vicar, *precisely because* they are 'not particularly religious'. A lay welcome that's too long can compound a couple's 'hypocrisy'. A warm and friendly vicar is the person they really need to meet for that sense of hypocrisy to be absolved. And that, as soon as possible.

A word about that word 'vicar'

One vicar told us of the day he was walking through the churchyard just after a service when a couple, shyly holding hands, approached. They asked: 'Are you the vicar?'

'Oh no', he instinctively replied, 'I'm the NSM.'

When we say *vicar* in the Weddings team, we are choosing to use a word that most people in England will use of anyone with a dog collar on within striking distance of an Anglican church. Because people in England usually use it, we do too.

People who don't go to church probably won't know the precise difference between an NSM, a rector and a curate, and why should they? The church's favourite term, clergy is a noun denoting a body of people. A single member of this body is either a clergyman or a clergywoman. Can you imagine if we wrote all through the website: 'your clergyman or clergywoman will help you'? Meanwhile, priest is more likely to communicate Catholic, and minister has a free church resonance. So in the Project we decided that, while it is not always technically correct to say vicar, we should say it anyway. We have judged that the Church of England will be more keen to seek a newcomer's comfort than their linguistic enlightenment.

When I was a communications officer in a diocese the first question journalists asked before an interview with the bishop was 'what should I call him?' And it's what your couples want to know too, about talking to you.

There's a scene in *EastEnders* when single mother Heather, meeting the vicar about her son's christening, alternately addresses him as 'your grace', 'your honour' and 'your holiness', and even exhibits an occasional nervous curtsy. We use this video in Weddings Project presentations to indicate our essential research case, that people are anxious about meeting a vicar, desperate to get it right, and deeply but simply reassured by being able to use the right term of address. So the Project has just cut through it all and called every ordained person a vicar. That goes for all our leaflets and online resources for couples. We do get occasional complaints about this from canons and team rectors, who may prefer that we point up the essential differences. But most vicars are happy to be described as such, and you might be too.

The vicar makes the difference

When the Weddings Project team took this news around the country in presentations – to clergy mainly, but to lay people too – there were smiles all round. Almost. One person reported:

> 'What surprised me was how important the role of the vicar was to them. I'd always thought they were a kind of necessity but not necessarily a wanted bit of it. It has massively encouraged me.'

One lay administrator admitted to a 'doctor's receptionist' approach: 'I never felt completely happy with the policy of keeping all but the difficult cases away from the vicar until he absolutely had to see them.'

A vicar said: 'I think I always knew deep down that wheeling me in six weeks before the wedding to help them choose the hymns isn't the best.'

On the other hand, one vicar reported back six months after the presentation about how the parish had taken the Weddings Project's research findings. He said, 'The lay people found it hurtful that meeting the priest was more important than meeting them.'

A vicar of one of the most marrying churches in England said: 'I agree with the truth of what you're saying. But I could never deliver the number of weddings I'm doing if I got too involved. Our lay team is first class and I couldn't do it without them.' The admittedly superb lay team in this church, though affirmed, saw it this way: 'The couples really do want more of the vicar than they are getting. We love this ministry but the couples need more of the things that only he can do for them.'

Our researchers said that vicars who are 'approachable but not too matey', reassure the public that they have found a person of goodwill in whom they can place their trust.

They can become a priestly friend, someone who can be their key contact point with the church while they plan their wedding. If this connection is well made, it speaks volumes about who the church is for and what it is about.

Tamar Kasriel, the Weddings Project's lead researcher, is not someone who has an axe to grind about the church one way or the other. She is a director of a research agency which is commercial and secular. Yet some of the research findings surprised her. Here is her message for England's clergy:

> 'I would want to say to the vicars, and I was surprised by this to some extent: people *really value you*. You make a huge difference to the way people feel, not just about their wedding day but I think about the Church in general. People do make this distinction between their local church, 'my church' and the Church with the capital C. And it's the vicars who make the difference.'

Most other people in the weddings world have a commercial motive, and work for a couple until the big day is done. But a vicar is perceived to have a more genuine motive; not transactional, but personal. And properly effected from the start, it's a human connection that really can live on after the wedding day.

Warmth is valued above all

Over the course of the Weddings Project the research team sent in regular dispatches. And one, concerning the ministry of the ordained, had this headline: 'Their warmth is what is valued above all.' Not exactly earth shattering. I think we'd always guess that a warm vicar is better than a cold one, generally, if you're thinking about the growth of the Church. But the research was beginning to *prove* something about vicars, even if we had always suspected it was true. Uniform matters. But the person inside it needs to have this one thing about them: human warmth. Tamar put it this way:

> 'Almost all the people we spoke to talked about how warm their vicars had been and how much difference that had made. Because couples are looking for a very human experience – they want *their wedding*. If they go to the big hotel or the register office they will be married by somebody they've never met before and they'll probably never see again.
>
> What the vicar is able to do is to make them feel that they are being married by someone they know – someone who knows them, and who can elevate the experience into something that has a humanity and warmth that really makes the difference.'

The possibility of getting to know your marrying priest and be known by them is what commercial consultants would call the Church's unique selling point in the weddings market. No one else offers it. We have been offering it for centuries. But the world has changed. Now, more often than not, the people coming for a wedding don't yet know who's inside the church. More than ever they come from very far away, with a historic connection to an area. What makes the difference to them coming to us, and staying with church thereafter? From the outset, it's the warmth of the vicar.

Having made this discovery about the value to mission of clerical warmth, we did consider inventing the Weddings Project *Warmthometer*, a kind of Geiger counter to assist at selection conferences or to try out on your deanery chapter colleagues. But warmth is not something you necessarily need to *feel* in order to radiate it. You communicate warmth by doing simple things well. You are acting warmly when someone leaves a message about their wedding and you respond without delay. Your warmth communicates through your posture and your tone of voice together with the words you choose. It communicates when you invite couples to call you by your first name. It communicates when you can show that you remember a few things about them. You could say that being warm is a decision you take.

One vicar told us: 'I just say "I love doing weddings. I love doing weddings." I say it when I meet the couple, at the rehearsal and in the sermon. I keep saying it. I say it so much I find that I have begun to believe it.'

One thing we found about warmth is that it's easiest to isolate it when it's *not* there. Listen to the words of one young man from our Oxford research sample:

> 'There was no warmth. He didn't say 'we're really pleased you want to get married in this church'. He sat back in his chair like an old schoolmaster and I thought – oh no – what's he going to ask me?'

This is a man whose latent hypocrisy immediately progressed to fear because of how the vicar *didn't* sit and what he *didn't* say. The absence of warmth is also noticed in the context of the service. This is from a man interviewed in a companion piece of work about funerals:

> 'The vicar who did the service, there was none of that *warmth* in his voice. You could tell he'd done it many times before.'

It was the amiable late Archbishop Robert Runcie who spoke of the 'sociability required of a priest'. And, given the clear recommendations of this particular research, we agree. Human warmth is the essential characteristic sought by unchurched people of ordained people. It is missionally astute for us as the Church in England to seek it out, affirm it, teach and train for it. Thus trained, we wisely position our vicars at the door and let them be the ones who are first in line to meet the world.

The warm vicar at the door

It was John Finney's research in the 1980s and summarised in his book, *Finding Faith Today* [Bible Society, 1992], which set out a foundation on which the Weddings Project has been building, even if unwittingly. This is what he writes in his chapter, 'The Minister'.

> People turn to him or her for baptisms, weddings and funerals unless they have a link with another church. Many come with virtually no church background, never having talked to a minister before and more than half expect a rebuff. If they find someone who is friendly, glad to see them, and helpful they are both relieved and impressed.

There is an almost eerie read-across to the research for the Weddings Project. Here's Tamar speaking two decades later:

> 'We found in the research that the vicar makes a huge difference to the wedding, to the way a couple feels about their wedding. Couples can be quite nervous when they first begin the whole wedding experience, they don't know what they are getting into. They may be quite nervous about going into a church ... it may have been a long time since they were last in one. The vicar is the person who can turn that into a positive and welcoming experience for them.'

Finney goes on to say that the friendliness of the ordained is the 'necessary beginning' for the most effective evangelism, which he defines as 'growing out of an existing pastoral relationship'. And his research bears this out: in six out of ten cases the priest – seen, not as a plaster saint but a human being – was identified as a reason or the reason why people became Christians. So when it comes to initial contact, it really helps if there's a warm priestly person to receive it. But if that is not possible, and the couple hears first from a lay person or an answer phone or sends an email, then the vicar should not take long to attend to the message personally. It matters for mission that they do. One lay administrator told us that she sees herself as the 'warm-up act' for the vicar, able to give couples reassurance that the vicar's 'really lovely' and the next conversation will be with her, and that it will go really well.

The more quickly contact is mediated from lay person to ordained, the more seriously you are taking the couple then the quicker their anxiety will melt away.

Do you know a vicar? If so, what are they like?

The Weddings Project felt as if it had walked through a door marked 'weddings' into a much bigger room, called 'the role of the ordained for the mission of the Church in the 21st century'. But we had to do a bit more checking first. The research team took a camera onto the streets of Salisbury to ask random passers-by a few questions. They wanted to know if people knew any vicars, and if not, what they would expect one to be like.

A middle-aged lady lit up with a beaming smile: 'Well he's called Father John and he's absolutely brilliant. It's very easy to get hold of him. I look on him as a friend but I suppose I'd need him for the happy things in life as well as the sad things, and just someone to talk to, which we do quite often.'

A young man said: 'To be a vicar I think you would have to be quite open minded – no problems, no scepticism – every time open minded to everyone.'

A woman said: 'I live in a place called Lee-on-Solent which is a small community and I knew the vicar very well because I lived almost next door to the church and he was very much part of the community. He had an open door policy, so he was available to us as parishioners at any time.'

An open door policy? 'And why would you need one?' they asked.

'To help me organise a funeral' said an older lady. 'Maybe if you're getting married', two sixth-form lads said in unison. 'Maybe he could give you a hand with something, spiritually or physically, just anything,' said one young man. And another said: 'Why would I need a vicar? I don't know, maybe if I was thinking about getting confirmed, or someone to share problems with ...'

These snippets from Salisbury confirmed the idea that the pastoral offices are the essential life-moments when the Church is actively sought by people who don't usually go. But more than that, people – especially young men according to our snapshot – say they would seek out a vicar for company as well as churchy reasons: 'just to talk to', as much as 'if I wanted to be confirmed'.

When we asked Salisbury where you would find a vicar if you wanted one, they were unanimous in expecting to find one in a church. 'On the way to school I pass easily five', said one. 'Small villages is where you'd find one, because every small village has a vicar', another said with certainty. 'I'd just go to the cathedral and ask them for one. I'm sure they'd point me in the right direction', said another. Like Postman Pat and his van, people expect the uniform to come with a vehicle. In England today most people expect to find a vicar in a church. It's that simple. They say that if they needed one, and they would for a wedding, then they would just pop in.

The uniformed professional on the outside edge of the organisation

This apparent national openness to the uniformed professional at the point of public need made us wonder if other professions knew this too. After all, it could be part of a wider phenomenon the truth of which you may already know yourself. You may find it reassuring to see the 'bobby on the beat', and if you go to hospital you may long for the good old days of the matron on the ward. You may prefer banks to have bank managers rather than faceless call centres. Is this just sentiment or is there a deeper principle at work? And what do other professions do to keep their professionals in full public view?

Our enquiries took us to the headquarters of Lincolnshire police, to interview Chief Constable Richard Crompton, who leads on the 'bobbies on the beat' strategy nationally. He painted a picture of an advanced and sophisticated England that, at its heart, is still deeply traditional. He said:

> 'I think over the last three to four decades, the public's regard for the institutions, certainly policing, yes the Church, the banks, maybe the health service, has taken a bit of a battering. In some cases for good reasons, but for less good reasons too. And the world has changed, completely. There's

freedom of information, 24-hour news, everything we do and say now is reported in an instant so the scrutiny organisations are under is intense.

At the same time what I hear from the public is a longing for what they perceive to be the Dixon of Dock Green era, when the local bobby was a pillar of the community whom everybody knew, and there was a perception of closeness which they mourn. They would love that to come back.

People do have very strong affiliation to, a longing for those reassuring elements of the community, the police officer, the vicar. If they go into a hospital they want to see someone who looks and sounds like a nurse. It gives them reassurance and some faith that they are going to be dealt with correctly.'

On one of the Weddings Project presentations one priest reflected that we live in a visual culture where icons communicate strongly, and the Church can work with that since the dog collar gives the church instant public recognition. Yet one young curate, turning up at his first staff meeting wearing his dog collar, was told 'we don't do that round here', and he never wore it again except for high ceremonial occasions.

At the door virtually all the time

So the Weddings Project takes the view that the warm vicar at the door makes a difference. In other words, it matters for mission that the vicars in your church are identifiable, warmly disposed to people and easily available to the public when required. We came to that view because of what research found out. And if it's true, what would you need to change to make room for it? You may say this would be a nice view to take in George Herbert's world, with one priest per church and a modestly populated parish. But you don't need me to tell you those days are long gone. How can you be 'at the door' of eight or ten rural churches at once?

Well, George Herbert's world had its limitations. He only had a horse to get around with. Through your parish website you can easily be in ten places at once. Your website is saying something right now, for better or worse. It might be cluttered, it might be didactic, it might be inviting, or you may not have one. Whatever it is or isn't, it is communicating something. That some-thing is either pulling people towards your church or pushing them away. What is the value of your website to today's marrying generation? It's a really smart tool to use if you want to 'meet people where they are', as we tend to say a lot in the Church of England. Today's bride is about 30, and going online to find things out is natural to her. She's afraid to pick up the phone to you, and she also feels hypocritical about choosing church for a wedding. Precisely because of that she feels more comfortable to check you out without you knowing, and your website lets her do that. Plus, she'll feel a bit better briefed for any preliminary encounter.

In the world of writing online, less is more. People scan, they browse, they are impatient to get to the bit they need. They don't like to be presented with too much information, since it requires more sifting. While you may say that for us in the church, when it comes to words more is more, it is not so for your couple, looking in. Fewer words mean more to them, so ruthlessly reduce your word count. White space and pictures draw the reader in. In the best of all possible worlds, your weddings page only need have five elements. Like this:

1. We love doing weddings here!
2. Get in touch with the vicar – here's how.
3. Our vicar's name is [first name not initial]
4. And our vicar looks like this: [warm, and wearing a dog collar]
5. For loads more about weddings see www.yourchurchwedding.org

The point of providing a link to the national weddings website is that *we* can do all the writing which is common to all parishes, like the law, and make the necessary changes so that you don't have to. You can just use your site to encourage contact, and link to us for all the national detail. The Weddings Project has produced free banners which you can use to link your site to ours. Find these at www.yourchurchwedding.org/project

When we did our research in 2008 the lion's share of first contact went to the phone, at 63%, with email at 7%. Judging from our tour of England, phone is still the bride's favourite but some churches report that the split is nearing half and half. Brides and grooms are more likely to contact you about a wedding if your website communicates a very few essential things. Who the vicar is and what she/he looks like are two of those things. By giving your vicar an online profile you are putting him or her at the door of the church, virtually. And if you have more than one church, your vicar is at all the doors at once.

Theological training and the best place for the priest

You're down at the bottom of the page and perhaps you're expecting to read some reassuring caveats, such as every member ministry is a Kingdom principle. It is. The newest Christian is as much an ambassador of Christ as the Archbishop of Canterbury. Yes, that's true. And yet, we are bringing you the news that at this particular life moment, the ministry of the ordained is particularly sought, and *their* warmth is particularly felt as grace. It may not be an eternal value. But it's true for the current generation of marrying couples. You may already know it, but it may be a challenge for you to make room for it. You are busy enough already and, if you do choose to make room for this, it may affect your marriage ministry from top to bottom, in practical ways that you may not have considered.

If you agree it's true and you want to go this way, it will not require you to lay off all lay assistance in this ministry. A vicar's personal intervention is only required at seven moments between the first phone call and the first anniversary. Research shows that at these particular moments couples are surprised and delighted to receive priestly contact, and the kind of contact that works for them is very easy to initiate with the things that the Weddings Project has to offer. All this means that if you are a vicar who wants to grow the Church through the ministry of marriage, you have all the tools you need, and only seven key moments you really need to attend to.

We are at the first moment, when contact is first initiated. The next will be when you and this couple meet for the first time.

Secret summary

✓   **Make it easy for couples to get in touch.** Make sure your vicar is the main contact on your page on www.achurchnearyou.com and that the church's listing is up-to-date and informative.

✓   **Look at your church notice board and parish website if you have one.** Is your vicar known by an initial or a first name?

✓   **Know the law.** Go to www.yourchurchwedding.org/project and download the simple guide to the law. Keep it where it will be close to hand when you deal with initial enquirers.

✓   **Ensure your fees and charges and legal, clear and reasonable.** Look at the 1,2,3 guide to setting fees and charges and check that you follow this.

Moment Two:
The First Meeting

A church that doesn't delay before moving to moment two and meets a couple soon after they call communicates a lot with a little effort. A quickly arranged first meeting takes a nervous couple's seriousness seriously. It makes the most of the time you have with them.

- **The vicar makes the difference, but you may have more than one to call on. In which case, who is the best one to meet them?**

- **Where is the best place to meet?**

- **What is the right information to give them, so early on in the journey? What do they need if they live far away?**

- **Is it actually possible to get all you need to know about a couple on to two sides of A4?**

_____

All that we have found out about vicars matters for this first meeting moment, just after a couple is first in touch. But research pointed up the rather startling mismatch between some established church practices and the preferences of the couples who come for a wedding. They are not feeling at home. Not being, as they say it, 'particularly religious', nevertheless they come with a desire for God to bless their marriage. They may be half thinking they won't be allowed it.

I write as a person who has run lay welcome teams for churches which have been fun, smart and effective. But the fact is this. No matter how fabulous and talented your lay colleagues, no matter how friendly or organised or helpful they are compared to you, and no matter your favoured ecclesiology:

The couple wants to meet the priest who will conduct their wedding – as soon as possible.

You will get a sense of this if you work on Church of England stands at Wedding Shows around the country. Of course, it is still fairly surprising to see the Church in a trade fair environment, and at one the cry was heard: 'Hey Maureen, come over here, I can see a guy dressed as a vicar.' It is common for clergy who staff these stands to be asked by passing brides-to-be to conduct their wedding – when people meet a warm vicar they do not want to let them go. Couples who have booked their wedding in church and then see the Church of England at a Wedding Show do sometimes communicate a sense of not knowing what will happen to them next. This limbo couples feel is usually because their marrying priest has not yet been assigned to them, and this can reinforce any pre-existing sense of unworthiness they may have.

One member of the Weddings Project team had to go into hospital for minor surgery, and he experienced the same phenomenon. First of all he was called to a meeting with a very friendly nurse who told him all that was about to happen and who the surgeon would be. At a subsequent meeting he met the registrar, who was also very courteous, called him 'Sir' and asked him if he would appreciate the services of a chaplain. Very good. But all through this process, the patient is thinking, 'Where's the person who's actually going to wield the knife?' In that lay his anxiety. It wasn't until the day of the operation, and just a few moments before it, that he did meet the surgeon, and cried out: 'I know you!' It turned out that he did know him, from a completely different context. 'I can't tell you how much of a relief it is to know I'm in the hands of someone I know,' he blurted out.

The Weddings team has found this sort of idea makes sense because churches are already finding it is true in real life. One lay administrator said to us:

'It's true that there is a special hush that comes over the couple when the vicar is in the room, a sort of respect. When he's not there they talk much more naturally, much less guardedly, they ask different questions. All of that does actually mean that when it comes to talking seriously about the most serious day of their life, it's got to be with the person who will conduct their wedding.'

Now, of course this can lead to difficulties in churches where the wedding goes in the diary with 18 months' notice and the vicar's summer holiday goes in the diary six months later. We know from vicars and couples that, having made a connection, the pain of breaking it is very real. It is a sign that what we are saying is true, and you may have noticed yourself that couples do quickly get 'glued' to their vicar. It is very difficult then to break that bond and try to re-create it with another. If it feels uncomfortable to do this, it's because it's actually hurting the couple if you do.

In order to get round this, or at least postpone it, some churches get the couples in groups to brief them about the practical commonalities of getting married at the church before they have their vicar assigned to them. But many do sense the huge amount of lingering anxiety in the couple at these meetings, about who their vicar will be and what the first meeting will be like.

To assign a couple to their marrying priest up front and early reduces their anxiety and makes the most of the period of time you have with them, precious time for mission.

This 'grip' in which vicars are held by the couples whose weddings they conduct is not hero worship. It is not sinful. It should not, at least in the early stages, be discouraged. It is just what couples need to do to feel at ease in this foreign and frightening environment when what is at stake is the most important day of their lives. Their marrying priest becomes an essential component of how they feel about their wedding day.

Have we been introduced?

Around the country we met vicars who, on hearing this, said it is utterly impossible, but we also met vicars who said it is utterly possible. One said: 'Because we are in a team, there's just no way we can match up the couple with their marrying priest as early as when they book the wedding.' While another told us, 'Because we are in a team, we just assign the vicar to the wedding on a cab rank principle; whenever a new wedding comes in we assign it to the next one in line!'

Of course it may happen that it is not possible to do a wedding that you had hoped to do and to which you were committed. If it does, we recommend that the handover be enacted relationally. If you can make a couple feel that they are being introduced to a 'friend of yours', it will help them.

We can only repeat what the research found out: that a vicar is a vicar is a vicar. The public do not see our ecclesiastical distinctions. And whether it is to be the curate, the bishop or the supermarket chaplain who will conduct their wedding, they want to meet them as soon as possible. Accepting this desire and going with it does actually maximise the time you have with each couple, so it's a good thing to do if you want to grow your church through your weddings ministry.

Everybody's got a kettle

The fear of meeting the marrying priest is as pronounced as the desire to meet her or him. That's because of the importance of the event, the store that is set by it, and the guilt that the whole idea tends to generate in couples who feel unequal to the meeting. Bishop of Jarrow, Mark Bryant puts it this way:

> 'This is very, very *scary* stuff. Is the vicar going to tell us off because we don't go to church? Is he going to make us come to church? Is he going to tell us off because we've been living together? Should we let on that we've got children already? This is very scary.'

If having children is a barrier to making contact, people are still reluctant to admit it by the moment of first meeting. We met one couple in Yorkshire who stumbled upon a beautiful abbey church on a day out, and later found it to be inhabited by a wonderful vicar who welcomed them with open arms. Six months later they were still wondering whether to mention to him that they had two sons.

Lots of vicars already plan for the fear factor by arranging to meet couples on the couple's own home turf, where the existence of children might be more easily spotted. But in any case, giving thought to where you meet is time well spent. Archdeacon Emeritus John Barton is part of the Weddings Project team and is someone who, in his long ministry in the Church of England, has advised the media on how to interview bishops and vice versa. His advice, never to be interviewed in front of book cases, from behind the barrier of a desk or inside yawning echoing empty churches, holds in every area of public relations. Including where to meet your couple for the first time.

What does it make couples feel when they see you framed by your wall-to-wall book cases crammed with all those impenetrable tomes, all of which you will undoubtedly have read? It makes them feel like you are clever and they are not. It heightens the sense of difference between you. What about if you take them into your well-kept 'visitors only' living room, would that be better? We heard of how one bride, perched on the edge of the vicar's sofa in one such splendid vicarage reception room, gawped with wonder saying: 'Do you really live here?' So in the Weddings Project we say, do pay attention to all the things that are necessary to safeguard you and your family, if you have one, where you work. But after that, consider where to meet the couple so that they would feel most at ease. It may not be the kitchen, but everybody's got a kettle. Find a place to meet that minimises the differences between you, not exaggerates them. In so doing, you will show God's own acceptance and welcome to a couple who are feeling nervous, anxious and frightened to put a foot wrong.

Give a gift

At Weddings HQ there are stacks of graphs showing what most couples are offered at this first meeting, and what they would prefer to receive. The overall impression of what was offered in two dioceses where we carried out some research was more technical or transactional than inspirational. So, for example, couples were more likely to get electoral roll, banns and fees information than hymn choices or photography tips or the reasons why marriage is good for you.

To help with this, the Project team produced what has become the centrepiece of its resources: a ribboned *Welcome Folder* with ten leaflets that breathe inspiration. It's designed to be at least as good as what a couple will get from the limo company or the reception venue, and contains facts and tips common to all churches (but there's room for you to add what's specific to yours). The welcome folder has been designed to appeal particularly to women, who adore it, although men think it's OK too. Over the time the church is in touch, cards and notes can be added to the folder, so it can grow into a souvenir keepsake of their time with you, all tied up with a bow. Clergy from dioceses participating in the Project remark on how well these folders are going down. One vicar said, 'It's so helpful, to have something to take with me when I meet them – they say, 'Oh wow can I keep this?' – and something to leave with them. It feels as if the church is still communicating welcome after I've left the building.' When it was reported that a bride in the North East cried when her vicar offered this gift, the bishop, who understood exactly what was going on, promptly ordered a load more. It's good to hear that what's offered in churches touches hearts.

Copies of the *Welcome Folder* are now available for anyone to buy direct from Church House Publishing (www.chpublishing.co.uk or 01603 785923), as well as via participating dioceses. So give a gift when you meet your couple for the first time, and let it be something that speaks of inspiration. In doing so, you may give the gift of grace to someone who didn't expect it.

Referral

Some clergy in Bradford and Oxford were unmoved by the idea of the 2008 Marriage Measure as a potential aid to mission. After all, if more couples were to be marrying far away from where they live, how are they supposed to stick with church after the day? The team really had to listen to this tension: the heartbeat of the Measure is to welcome more weddings, but encouraging more weddings far from home could counteract post-wedding 'stickability'. How many couples do marry outside their parish of residence anyway? And how do we care for them well?

Research among couples marrying in Bradford and Oxford before the Marriage Measure indicated that about four in ten were marrying 'away'. This could be just in the neighbouring parish, but it could involve greater distance than that. By now it will be at least 50%, but even that figure was thought to be far too low by vicars in dioceses like Truro and Carlisle. A significant proportion of the weddings the Church of England does are for people who live outside our parish. Cracking the problem of long-distance care led us back to the ancient art of 'referral'.

People tell me referral was once taught at theological colleges as an essential ministry discipline – ironically when the nation was less mobile than it is now. As a matter of course a vicar in a parish where someone was moving on – usually to university or to college – would alert the chaplain there to a potential warm and sympathetic contact. So, could reviving the practice of referral help us in a post-Marriage Measure world? If it's really scary to meet one vicar, what's it like to meet two? Yet a good connection with the vicar is just what a couple needs to help them 'stick' at home. Could the marrying priest help effect it? We asked vicars in Bradford and Oxford if they would be willing to help the couples they marry by tracking down their home vicar for them. And here's what some of them said:

'How would I know how to contact their home parish? It's onerous and problematic.'

Someone who wasn't fond of Somerset for some reason, said: 'I don't want to have to chase around Taunton looking for their parish church – it's their problem.'

And someone who saw the problem as one which could inspire missionary endeavour, said: 'At least if the onus is with them, they stand a chance of connecting with their home parish.'

Eventually it came down to this: 'Clergy have enough to do anyway.'

Now, some clergy do refer couples to their parish church, and good for you if you do. You can do this at the first meeting by entering their postcode into www.achurchnearyou.com and up should pop the parish church details. You can print this and give it to the couple who take it home with them to initiate contact there. On the other hand we heard a range of curious alternative practices – one vicar admitted to referring couples to their local funeral directors instead because 'they know the local parishes best'. It's never been the Weddings Project's intention to lay more expectations on hardworking clergy, and we don't aim to change the law either (the onus is on the couple to find their parish of residence if they need their banns read there). But mobility is a reality and sometimes online data is inadequate, and over all these things a good connection with the home vicar may enhance the conditions for 'stickability' at the home church after the wedding.

So the Weddings Project is offering to be the middle man, and has been testing a referral service so you can send a couple to us if they need help to find their home parish. We'll alert their home vicar of the couple's interest, tell the couple who it is, and tell the marrying priest too, so everyone knows about each other. The presenting need for banns will probably give a couple their first experience of their local church. We're working with vicars to effect that encounter quickly, simply, personally and warmly. More than that, we're offering invitations to support it: invitations to the reading of their banns to come from the church where they live – as well as where the wedding will be. Do refer a couple to us by giving them our email address (weddings.project@ churchofengland.org) and we will be in touch with them – and you – about their warm local vicar.

Banns and workload

The Weddings team hopes that this careful 'twinning' will result in more couples finding the love of their home church as soon as possible and sticking there after their big day, even if it is very far away from where their wedding will be. Now you may be a vicar who struggles to see the potential in 'banns couples'. Ask yourself this: How likely is it for our terminology to frame our expectations, and for our expectations to be self-fulfilling? How does it feel as a 'banns couple' to be directed to the 'vestry hour' when they can meet the churchwardens who will 'do all the paperwork'. How comprehensible and inviting does that sound? But most vicars are delighted to have a warm lead to two parishioners who have a real and happy reason to be looking for their parish church. We in the Weddings Project love it when we sense in the referred vicar delight at receiving a meaningful contact like this. With quicker contact and supported by specialist invitational resources, they and we have faith that such a couple could be part of the churchgoing congregation by the time of their wedding.

Does she want to convert me?

We did meet a vicar just like this – we never discovered her name. We found her when we found brides talking in an online chatroom about vicars they'd met. A bride was telling the story of how she rang her home vicar about her banns and ended up talking on the phone for 40 minutes. The two women immediately arranged to meet. First of all the bride was pleased to have found a vicar who was so interested in her and how she'd met her groom (H2B in chatroom shorthand). But later she had second thoughts. Concerned, she said to the other brides, 'Maybe she wants to convert me?'

The others reassured her: 'Don't worry, vicars never want to convert you!'

After the meeting, the bride came back to the chatroom with a thoughtful update. 'Funny. In the end *I* was the one asking all the spiritual questions.'

The paperwork

One thing that came through loud and clear from vicars is how difficult it is to keep neat records about the couples you're marrying. What is really needed, clergy said, is one single piece of paper that captures everything you need to know about each couple. Some determined churches were designing their own, but most churches were still using the SPCK-produced 'banns application form'. Burgeoning filing cabinets are never good, and so, with the aim of making life easier for churches, we put the Weddings Project's designers onto it. Their task: to get everything that is legally required and generally useful for a couple's wedding onto two sides of A4. They did it, and we put the form online and waited to see the response. We make it freely available so you can download it and print it out in Project lilac or in a black and white version if you like. You can even edit and save it to your PC now and not print it out at all.

What really worked was that vicars began to use it, and then got in touch to thank us and ask for various other developments to make it even more useful. We are so indebted to this incremental community upgrading. Because of it we know that our online form is legally current and actually useful across the Church of England. What's online is always the latest version. Find it at: http://justforvicars-yourchurchwedding.org/resources/downloads

Only one thing has been lost, and that's the layout. We just couldn't get everything on and retain the 'certificate' style layout, which is what people really liked about the SPCK form and which (some said) reduced errors in the transfer of names over to the final marriage certificate. But we've stopped trying now: if this form helps you, then please do use it, and if it doesn't please don't. The form itself has no particular status in law and there is therefore no compulsion to use any particular one. (If you still like to use the SPCK version, you don't need me to tell you it is out of date. And it features a box about baptism – unhelpfully since it is not a legal requirement.)

Form filling and emotional intelligence

So this is one way to make your life easier. However, the key aim of the Weddings Project is not to make your life easier, but to help you to care for couples so well that more of them stick with church after the day. That's why we have designed the form the way we have – streamlining your systems is incidental – in the great cause of growing the Church of England. Let me explain. If you put this form in the post, or ask the couple to fill it in, or leave it at the back of church or whatever, you have given something away that you can never get back. You've declined to sit with this couple and talk to them in the secondary task of gleaning necessary information from them. Because this form is not just a form, it is an aid to this initial and primary 'get to know you' session.

Imagine that you were meeting the surgeon about an operation you were about to have. If you were emailed the forms to fill in, how reassured would you feel about what was about to happen to you? Would you feel better going through all the details with your surgeon there, so that you knew for sure they had it all down right? It's that important. All couples understand that there is paperwork involved. But they are worried about meeting you, they do not know anything about church law and they are frightened of getting something wrong. When you take the strain on the opening admin, they feel reassured and comforted. They can ask the questions that only you will know the answer to. They will feel as if they are being served by you, as they are, and you get to know them a bit better too. Because we dream that every one of these forms is filled in by a vicar in the context of getting to know a couple who is present, it is 'vicar facing' in the way it is written, and not littered with every conceivable legal detail which vicars would know or could look up later. And because it's for the vicar to fill in with the couple there, it intentionally uses the words we know great vicars use in this necessary process of getting down all the information.

For example, early on in the process we dispensed with the term 'application form' as we thought it was a pretty mean idea that marriage in the Church of England is something you apply for. Feeling 'hypocritical', the word 'application' can reinforce in a couple's minds that they are unequal to the transaction. Because this word is so unhelpful, we have replaced it, so it's a *Welcome and Congratulations* form instead. These are the words your couple needs to hear from you. These are the words they need to hear from a Church of England which longs to help them find themselves at home. And in this great quest, little things, like the manner and vocabulary of our form filling, can make a big difference.

Secret summary

✓ **Assign a couple quickly to their marrying priest** and let that person be the couple's principle point of contact. This reduces anxiety and the feeling of being in 'limbo'.

✓ **If there are other people in the church that can help them,** introduce them personally.

✓ **Make sure you meet them in a place that helps them feel comfortable.** Consider meeting in your kitchen rather than your study, or on their home turf rather than yours.

✓ **Say congratulations.** It might be your 100th wedding, but it might be their first.

✓ **Say you love doing weddings.** They may feel they are being a bother to you.

✓ **Don't forget that your posture communicates.** Sitting forward in your chair communicates interest.

✓ **If they seem overconfident,** remember this too may be the product of a fearful mindset.

✓ **Refer them to their home church.** If you find this difficult email us at weddings.project@churchofengland.org and we can do it for you.

✓ **Filling in the forms together helps you get to know them.** If you delegate this, or ask them to do it themselves, you may not be communicating interest in them.

✓ **Give a gift when you first meet them.** Let it be something that will go on inspiring them long after the meeting has ended, such as …

✓ **If you haven't already seen one, get hold of the Welcome Folder.** This will provide you with something to give the couple now and also cards to mark other significant moments along the church wedding journey.

Moment Three:
Space to Think

The Church, unique among wedding venues, sets preparation as a high priority. No one else in the wedding marketplace offers time and space to think about the days after the wedding. Today's couples reach the altar older, and in many ways wiser, than generations before, and churches wonder how to respond to this with an invitation that makes sense.

- **Where is a couple's natural focus?**

- **What words work well when we invite them? What words don't sound inviting to them?**

- **How do you know whether what you offer really helps?**

- **How do you really know that they enjoy it?**

- **How much ministry time should this realistically take?**

- **What will really help a couple keep their vows for life?**

Prepared – for what?

The Weddings Project is not a marriage preparation project, although that is one of the things it found out about along the way. What the Project wanted to do, for the Church of England and all parties interested in marriage-care ministry, was to bring news of what people really think and feel about some of the Church's default settings and it didn't take long to get the picture. When it comes to 'marriage preparation', some things haven't changed for a long time. First, what we call it.

Let's recall what's going on with most couples today. Most of them are living together, have a mortgage together, manage a household budget, have 'in laws', and have lived through domestic harmony and conflict. Many of them will have learned some serious life lessons already – indeed for some those experiences will have brought them to the point of wanting to marry. One in five couples – according to research in Bradford and Oxford – already has children. There are some things you just can't teach them.

An engaged couple today, uniquely in this generation, is aiming for marriage as a 'crown' on a relationship which has taken some knocks and thrived. They want to celebrate a love which has already proved itself to be trustworthy and true. Given all that, how does 'marriage preparation' – as a term – sound to them?

Couples said it sounded a bit like a classroom subject, not hugely inspiring or inviting, something that 'ought to be done' as a prelude to having their wedding in church. A little bit worthy and intrusive, albeit potentially good for you in the end. The very term tends to carry with it something of the aroma of cod liver oil. Preparation for the marriage isn't something you get unless you marry in a church, but only 1% of couples interviewed told our researchers that 'the marriage preparation support offered by the church' was the number one reason for choosing church over any alternative venue.

Some couples told us that the term tended to confirm their own sense that they had little to offer which the Church didn't already know. It seems to communicate scant recognition for the life couples have already lived. It tends to say to them: 'Put aside your life together to date. You haven't even started yet.' What we hadn't really bargained for is that many vicars think this too. Coming through loud and clear from 176 clergy in Bradford and Oxford is that 'prep' feels preppy. The term 'sounds a bit classroomy', they said, 'old fashioned', 'a bit 1950s'. Some even said, 'Can you think of anything better to call it? If you can, I'll call it that.' So we discovered from couples *and* clergy that the term was ripe for a revamp.

Research also uncovered a loss of confidence among churches about how to offer it. One vicar told us he had only just stood down the retired bank manager who had for years led a workshop on balancing domestic books. The church had recognised that this no longer scratched where people itched. Some told us, 'it's getting increasingly difficult to get couples to come to this'. Others were dismayed that all the ministry time and effort that went into preparing couples for marriage rarely resulted in attendance at church after the wedding. Some clergy alluded to a sense of inadequacy if they didn't put on week-by-week courses. Some had organised these across a deanery, diocese or with other denominations so as to provide something substantial. In a small number of cases, the marrying church and the home church were teaming up to offer preparation closer to where the couple lived. A tiny number of churches had chosen to outsource this ministry to secular relationship-care agencies. Add to this the practical realities of the Marriage Measure.

So how best do we serve couples living far away? And what would couples find inviting? When we invite them to what we offer, what, if anything would they prefer to receive?

Our researchers asked newly married couples, looking back on how they were prepared from a point after their wedding, 'When it came to preparing you for your marriage, what were you offered by the church and what would you have been interested in?' They were given various options and could choose any combination of 'offered' and 'wanted' across a range. Some strong and surprising findings emerged.

The first is what came bottom of the list – the mode of preparation couples were least interested in, but which was apparently also least offered in churches. It was described as 'a week-by-week course about marriage'. While 11% of couples said they were offered this, only 9% said they were interested in it.

Now of course, some of the best-known resources in the Church are like this: weekly in regularity and modular in content. The Weddings Project greatly esteems the work of the people who produce these, and indeed all the stakeholders in this area, and we have worked closely with them through the life of the Project. If they have done any end-user research we have been grateful to see it, to check it against the 822 people we were speaking to about their experiences. For example, how had it felt to newly wed Steve to be offered a week-by-week course about marriage?

> 'I think it was every Wednesday night for six or eight weeks. And we went along and we watched a video and talked about some things and then we watched some more of the video and talked about more stuff. There were about ten couples there, some of whom were taking it seriously, some of whom weren't really interested but they were told they had to be there in order to get married there. So it was a bit of a bizarre experience really. I think I would have preferred something a little more personal rather than being sat in front of a telly and having a video played at you. It was an unusual kind of environment really.'

Steve and his bride found faith through their wedding, so Steve's words come to us with the attitude of a critical friend. His interview produces a ripple of wry smiles when we play it at Project presentations. There's a certain irony in the fact that Wedding Project events are just like this: playing some videos and talking about stuff. The point is that the adult learning environment might really suit us in the Church. But our research caused us to ask whether this necessarily works for everyone. They are asking for something 'more personal'. So does one size fit all anymore, if it ever did?

You can see in Steve's comment the hypocrisy which unchurched couples feel (*'they were told they had to be there in order to get married there'*). It is of course unlawful to compel any couple to meet a requirement beyond the demands of the law, so elaborate preparation events may be offered but cannot be insisted upon. Meanwhile Canon Law sets out the minister's duty to explain the doctrine of Christian marriage. So how can we do that, while meeting a couple's desire for 'something a little more personal'? Where is their natural interest when it comes to getting ready to be married in church?

The Weddings Project's researchers were greatly illuminated by what men like Steve told them. Men are generally less talkative on the subject of love and marriage, as we have established, but the evidence is that they are no less serious for that. Men do approve of the idea that churches offer preparation. They tend to understand it in vehicular terms, so in the same way that a car would have an MOT, they do feel it's right to have some sort of external 'check' that they are doing the right thing. When it comes to marriage preparation, they definitely think it should happen. They just don't think it should happen to them.

When it comes to talking about deep stuff with a stranger, men – in particular – resist. They do not feel that some stranger has the right to go about delving into their life and asking questions. And so some men, torn between wanting to do the right thing but experiencing deep discomfort, decide to go along with the process. In the words of one groom, 'You might just tell the vicar what you think he wants to know.'

It's very difficult to dig deep with men unless a genuine personal connection is established with the person doing the digging. Moreover for both men and women, lack of language is an issue. Yes, they are serious about God, but they feel inarticulate and that can make them feel out of their depth. Steve put it this way:

> 'If you expect everyone who walks through the door of a church to love God already – it's like expecting everyone who turns up at a French class to speak French fluently.'

Women may exhibit greater openness in the discussion of feelings. Indeed, they tend to describe spirituality using the language of feelings. But they still lack confidence in their ability to talk about God. Here's how a young bride from Bradford put it:

> 'We don't go to church, but it felt right at that first meeting that this is where we should get married. I don't know if that's kind of spiritual or not.'

Many women and men, serious about their marriage in church before God, can feel linguistically ill equipped and therefore uncomfortable. They might agree to what you offer them to prepare them, but they might just be doing it to please you and out of their own 'hypocrisy'.

What then can we offer that will put them at ease and start where they are?

The most wanted

Our research gave us two big clues, and these were in the two areas where the gap really does open up between what churches offer and what couples would prefer to receive.

Runner up in the 'most wanted' league, was this: 'a single-session course about marriage', more wanted (30%) than offered (22%) in churches in Bradford and Oxford. But what led the field in our research with couples was 'an opportunity to think about our wedding service and the vows we were making to each other'. More couples said they wanted this (43%) than felt they were offered it (35%), and it was the most-wanted option altogether.

If we put these two high-scoring options together, we get a clear win for the single-session event with a focus on the marriage service and the vows. This chimes with what Nicky said to the BBC programme *Don't Tell the Bride*. Walking into a church in Worcestershire which had atmosphere, beauty, history and charm, she said: 'I couldn't choose a civil ceremony. I wouldn't believe the words.'

It makes perfect sense that people who are spiritually serious but wordless are very much helped by the offer of our liturgy. And it makes sense that a generation yearning for a 'crown' on a relationship seeks the highest and most noble declaration of love. They find it in the love of which the Church's liturgy speaks. So the marriage service is a gift to people today. It sets the bar on love reassuringly high, and it offers words for their wordlessness.

All this came together for the Weddings team when we watched pop princess Cheryl Cole on ITV's Piers Morgan show. She was talking about the end of her marriage to football star Ashley Cole. Whatever you think of Cheryl, she is an icon for women in their late 20s and early 30s, just the women who are coming to our churches for marriage. She described herself as 'euphoric, calm and happy' on her wedding day, and subsequently appeared pained and embarrassed about the fact that her marriage was over.

Piers Morgan asked her: 'Did you honestly believe then that this would last forever?' She replied: 'Oh, I would never have took my vows if I didn't. It's not a joke. It's not something you go into light-heartedly, and it's not something you go into thinking, if I feel differently later, it doesn't matter.'

Even if celebrity culture brings out the cynic in you, you must have noticed how Cheryl used that term 'light-heartedly' which is a clear echo of the preface to the marriage service. Cheryl was never more serious than when she took her vows, and she was devastated not to have been able to keep them.

This backs up what research has discovered: the vows are the couple's natural focus when they prepare for their marriage. To a generation of couples whose address and whose friends won't change as a outcome of their wedding, the vows are the point of transformation. The moment of promise is their crowning moment.

Starting where people are

Some people contest the premise that we in the Church should be so keen to offer couples 'what they are interested in', in the language of our researchers. In these days when so many marriages, like Cheryl's and Ashley's, end in divorce, they say that there is a need for basic relationship education and that the Church has traditionally and rightly offered this.

While marriage care or relationship education has not been the Weddings Project's focus, church growth has. The Project team has dared to believe that if you aim to grow the Church you will get that, and better marriages with it. Researcher Tamar says that for the vicar preparing a couple for their wedding, there is a complex dynamic which requires discernment, sensitivity and permission giving. You could say that it's less classroom subject and more of a dance.

> What the most recent research identified is that it's in the period leading up to the wedding that vicars can make the most difference. It's by starting on the practical discussions, which is what everyone is open to, and gradually earning the right, the permission, to move into more spiritual territory that they can build the human relationship with couples that can then extend after the wedding.

Tamar and her team saw the art of preparation as a personal and relational one, and the timeline as one that extended until a year after the day. The art is in discerning where people are up to and what they are comfortable with. Talking them through the meaning and movement of their marriage service is the most practical place to begin. It could move on from there, if you sense couples would appreciate this and if you know you have their permission, but it doesn't make any sense to overwhelm them with input they are not ready for out of fear that you'll never get to tell them after the wedding.

One of the vicars from the Weddings Project team was sitting with a couple to prepare for their wedding. He was talking them through their marriage service with the vows as a focus in the way suggested here. Something about one of the promises triggered something deep in the groom who was previously reluctant to speak. 'From that moment, the words just tumbled out of him', this vicar said.

The value of the vows is that couples don't see it as you trying to improve them or educate them. They see the promises as something they want to make, mean and keep, in the context of the choreography of their wedding service. If you begin here you will be offering something personal. You will have their undivided attention, and you will probably spend less ministry time here, to potentially greater gain.

This is the moment to thank the NCT, the UK's largest charity for parents, who've been helpful to the Weddings Project by sharing their quest to get mums-to-be to learn parenting skills. Eventually they made peace with the fact that young mothers are interested in the *birth* before the birth, and parenting after it. The art for the NCT and, on the basis of this research, for us in the Church, is to start with people's natural point of interest and focus, believing that your friendship need not end with the wedding.

You will see later how a well-established connection with the vicar, built through the necessary practicalities of the service, can blossom into permission to be in touch after the wedding.

But what should we call it?

'Marriage preparation' is a term not loved by clergy or couples. So what should we call it instead? It was a question that we asked couples about their wedding day that gave the needed inspiration. Four out of ten newly weds, looking back on their wedding day, agreed with this statement: 'We would have liked some time *alone as a couple on the day to reflect* on the significance of the promises we had made to one another.'

Many vicars already know that couples want space to think on the day, and offer it in the vestry or a side chapel just after the service while the photographer is getting everyone organised outside. But as a team we were very taken by the spirit of this finding. Given all the things a couple is keeping in mind on the big day, there is, for almost half of them, a desire for 'space to think'. They want time to linger together in the afterglow of the promise moment. In this vein one bride told researchers: 'I would have loved some time to walk on the beach with my new husband and consider what we had done that day.'

So we brought that inspiration into marriage preparation. The Weddings Project has called it *Space to Think* instead, and we've designed a single-session event which takes couples through the choreography of the marriage service, tracing its pattern from preface to prayers, and drawing out the God dimension along the way. It's written by Andrew Body, a vicar in Guildford Diocese and the author of many marriage-care resources for the Church of England. He's designed it as a session lasting two hours or so and you can find the relevant factsheet at www.yourchurchwedding.org/project. It's supported by an invitation card to a single *Space to Think* event, featuring the vows from *Common Worship* on the front of the card and a friendly invitation on the back.

Space to think: online

When the Weddings Project team took soundings from clergy in their deanery chapters in Bradford and Oxford there was one request which came through with a certain stridency: 'Can you do anything to make sure those couples bring back those wedding music CDs we lend them?' We tried to help with this dilemma, although perhaps not in the way that was hoped.

We have research evidence to show that allowing people freedom to choose elements in their service has certain benefits, most crucially increasing 'inclination to stick', the Weddings Project's crucial church-growth driver. More about that when we get to the Big Day itself.

Remember all that we know so far about the fear that couples feel, their 'hypocrisy' and wordlessness. Now we know what a powerful draw the vows are to a generation that wants to crown its love. Could encouraging them to get to grips with the elements of the service help them prepare for their wedding?

Determined couples could always do this. With a book of hymns and the marriage service they could begin to see and feel what their service could be like. Or if they went online they could find the marriage service on the Church of England website, and any search engine would throw up wedding hymns to sing in a whole span of churches from Pudsey to Peru. So why couldn't the Church of England build something that made it a bit easier for couples to see and choose elements of their service? How about giving the couples some hymns and readings, and the marriage service text, so they could begin to put their choices together for themselves, online? Perhaps that could help them feel empowered, informed and therefore welcomed and wanting to stay.

Research speaks, but you can't be sure you heard it right until you've built something on the basis of the things you've found out and let people have it. We began to draft out the main essentials for a simple online ceremony planner with the help of our web team and York Minster's Peter Moger, then Worship Development adviser for the Archbishops' Council.

It works like this. A bride goes online to www.yourchurchwedding.org and clicks on the big 'ceremony planner' banner on the front page. She doesn't need to register, she can just dive right in, listening to a selection of hymns or clicking on 'lyrics' to read the words. After she's chosen a hymn or two (up to four is possible), the next stage is to choose at least one reading from the Bible. If then she wants to save her choices she can, by registering her name, the groom's name and the name of their church. This secures their choices and merges them into the text of a typical *Common Worship* marriage service. The couple can then print off a copy – the whole thing or just a summary – and at any stage return to amend their choices if they want. You can see how it works by trying it out, or just see two sample ceremonies – a long version and a short one at http://yourchurchwedding.org/planner/

We launched this service with some trepidation since, being online, it was difficult to pilot just in Bradford and Oxford – we had to offer it to the world. Initial responses from our two pilot dioceses however were encouraging. Having spoken to couples, Tamar Kasriel said:

> 'They mentioned the website, in terms of choosing hymns, in terms of understanding what options they had. This was received very positively indeed.'

The figures speak for themselves. Three years into this innovation, 50% of Church of England weddings are drafted using this online option, and searches for wedding hymns are the way that most people find www.your churchwedding.org to start with.

Brides write to us and say how they love the Ceremony Planner, especially how it drops their names into the vows, which is an incidental benefit. 'It makes it feel real, seeing in black and white those words that you will say on the day,' one said. Knowing how key those promises are to articulating seriousness, to crowning love, to drawing people to a church wedding in the first place, we shouldn't be surprised that it's as popular as it is.

That it has been a runaway hit with brides is one thing. What would the vicars of England think of it? But praise has come from as far away as Truro, from where the Precentor of the Cathedral, Perran Gay sent unsolicited congratulations. 'The Ceremony Planner is an excellent innovation,' he wrote, explaining how he is the sort of vicar who, when he meets couples, does copy and paste the text of *Common Worship* from the Church of England website on to a word document, then type in a couple's choices of hymns and readings and print it for them to take home. Since couples can now do this themselves at home, he is freed up to talk to couples about the things that only he can.

After all, in this Marriage Measure world 50% of couples get married miles away from where they live, so the face-to-face time you have with them is extra precious.

Of course not everyone likes it, but from those who don't, the feedback is that it goes too far or it doesn't go far enough. Some clever churches are asking for a couple's Ceremony Planner choices to download straight into a church's online diary, so they or even the organist can just log in and see what choices a couple has made.

We're also often asked for entry and exit music to be added to the planner. We're open to this, but we haven't done it yet for a couple of reasons. One is that Widor's Toccata, which would be a hit for couples, is a challenge for many church organists. The other is the liking for pop music processionals (one bride asked for a Florence and the Machine hit, while another really wanted – but was too scared to ask for – 'Here Come the Girls' by the Sugababes). We don't want to inadvertently communicate to couples that classical choices are more Christian than others.

We are also asked to amend the *Common Worship* default according to the preferences of particular churches, ones that like to use the shortened Preface or put the register moment in a different place, for example. To this end, we do write the supporting blurb in such a way as to make clear that the Ceremony Planner produces a draft for discussion, and there will be certain features of a couple's special church that will mean some things will be different. In some ways we do rely on your priestly skill for this, and your patience with us as we try to make the basic building blocks of most marriage services clear to a wide and general audience. We hope that this also goes some way to explaining why we don't provide a BCP specific version of the Ceremony Planner. All the authorised versions of the marriage service are available to read at http://www.yourchurchwedding.org/your-wedding/marriage-services.aspx

Couples may be feeling acutely unequal to the task when it comes to thinking through their service, and the gift you give them is to communicate that this church is for them, and it's their wedding. If they feel it is their wedding, they feel it's their church. And if they feel it's their church, they are much more likely to come back again.

Secret summary

✓ **Make an invitation of it.** Couples need to know they are invited.

✓ **Avoid classroomy metaphors.** Old fashioned terms are a turn-off.

✓ **One size doesn't fit all.** Be alert to the real ministry needs in each couple even if it means more personal time with you.

✓ **Watch out for the quiet ones.** Men can prefer to leave the talking to the woman. If pressed they might just tell you what they think you want to know.

✓ **Start with the practical.** The marriage service is where their natural focus is. Begin there, and bring God in as you go.

✓ **Let them be inspired at home** by recommending the online ceremony planner.

✓ **Take it easy.** Start with less before the wedding and you may win the right to be in touch in a meaningful way after the day.

Movement Four: Reading the Banns

Underneath the rubble of centuries of ecclesiastical custom lies the fourth moment that matters. It will happen on three Sundays – not necessarily consecutive – sometime in the three months before a couple's wedding day. It might happen close to home as well as far away. It's a very technical concept with an odd sounding name. In spring it gives rise to a litany of name calling. It's likely to sound very dull to you if you go to church. And a little exotic if you do not.

- **What's the opportunity at this moment for the marrying church?**

- **Is it nothing but an inconvenience for the home church?**

- **Could this be the simplest invitation to church you will ever make?**

- **Can you make a connection between a congregation and a couple through the banns?**

Some vicars express incredulity that the ancient ecclesiastical tradition of banns still goes on. Who knows who anyone is in our communities any more, never mind whether someone has been married before, they say. This accusation, that banns are an unnecessary medieval throwback adding to the paper-pushing demands of parish ministry, is something the General Synod has considered as part of the deliberations that brought about the Marriage Measure. They had considered doing away with them altogether, or posting them online instead of reading them out in church. But banns, albeit with a little bit of marginal tinkering by ecclesiastical committees, are here to stay.

On the other hand, nearly all the vicars we met in Bradford and Oxford took the opportunity to pray for couples when they read their banns. When they do, they use the banns prayer from *Common Worship*:

> Lord of love, we pray for this couple. Be with them in all their preparations and on their wedding day. Give them your love in their hearts throughout their married life together. Through Jesus Christ our Lord. Amen.

But it became clear that the couples in question were not often there to experience this. And the reason for that is that they hadn't often been invited.

From the couple's point of view, being invited to the reading of their banns makes perfect sense. First of all, it's an invitation to do with them and their wedding, and that is where their focus is. Second, the medieval thing doesn't bother them at all, they can see it as a little mysterious and compelling. The very idea is a little enigmatic, but in a culture which loves Dan Brown and Harry Potter, this can prove something of a draw.

More than that, you are actually inviting them to an opportunity to go to the place where they will marry, to get a feel for that place and be prayed for by all the people there. Why wouldn't you want to do this on a Sunday morning a month or two before your wedding, and go out for lunch together afterwards? It is a very special occasion on the road towards a wedding day, and couples can know that they are walking that road with the love and prayers of their church surrounding them.

Women expressed their delight at receiving such an invitation:

> 'They did some lovely things, like sending us a card about our banns and praying for us in church ... that was a really nice touch ...'

Men were a lot more straightforward in their appreciation. One said:

> 'I was really chuffed to be sent that.'

More usually with men, the invitation to come to church before the wedding makes sense precisely because they are feeling hypocritical. They are pleased to have some way of demonstrating their seriousness to you. One young man told his friends while researchers looked in:

> 'We had to go a few times before marrying there. It's nice. You should show an interest, you shouldn't just use them as a place to get married.'

Our researchers were amazed to find the deep experiences ushered in by this apparently unpromising formality, as was one man who described himself 'in the sceptic camp'. This is what he said happened when he took up the vicar's invitation to come and hear his banns read on Easter Day:

> 'I found something I really wasn't expecting: something the reverend said really struck a chord. My wife calls it my 'spiritual awakening'. It's something I'd like to go back and follow up on.'

We've since found out so much more about banns from vicars around the country that we are convinced this is as simple an invitation to church as you are ever likely to make and one that can have profound effects on the people who come. One vicar in St Albans Diocese told of how she went to hear her banns read. Then, she was someone who didn't usually go to church and she was experiencing at the time some great difficulties in her life. She found herself drawn back again and again to this church, during the quiet daytime hours when the church was open. Who could have guessed that the invitation to the reading of her banns could have set off a train of events that would one day lead to her ordination?

Of course, the marrying church isn't the only one that can make this special invitation. In about 50% of cases the home church is also reading the banns for couples marrying elsewhere. This can be an opportunity for the home parish to get to know a couple living in their parish even if the wedding won't be there. Couples may appreciate an invitation from their local church if they can't easily make the trip to hear their banns read where they will marry. In any case, couples need to know that they are invited. Anecdotally we've heard that the couple may be embarrassed that they didn't choose their local church to marry in. But because they are people who feel hypocritical, they do not naturally assume they can just come in.

So banns are the first real moment when home and marrying churches can team up to care for one couple. That's why the Weddings Project has produced a banns invitation card designed to be posted from the home as well as the marrying church, if they are different, and a friendly referral service to connect one church to another.

One vicar from a busy town centre parish wanted creative ideas for reading the banns, as in high season she found she had so many. She was keen to help make the experience special and personal for every couple if their names were buried in a list of many others. Meanwhile, researchers turned up the story of one couple, connected under the Measure, who felt 'blanked' by the vicar when they came to have their banns read.

We found a possible solution in one church in the West Midlands, which asks every couple for a photo when they read their banns, and projects their picture onto a screen for the congregation to see. This might help as a memory jogger for the vicar. But also the church community sees what they look like, and can make meaningful contact if they see them in or out of the church at a later date. The Midlands example, which has been commended nationwide now by the Weddings team, has a final flourish for after the service. The youth group makes it their business to seek out the couple and go to the front of the queue to collect their coffee order.

Across the country, we've found that asking for a photo in this way is not a difficult request, and of course couples need not supply one if they would rather not. So if you have the facilities where you are, you might consider this as a way of making more of the banns.

The other thing that churches are conjuring with is when exactly to read them. Some churches have abandoned the practice of putting banns at the start of the service with the rest of the notices, and now read them later, at the beginning of the intercessions, so that the prayers flow naturally from there. They have found that couples who are unfamiliar with church and who aren't sure of location, entry points or parking may arrive a little late and miss their banns moment if it's too early on.

Of course, you may be a church that does weddings mostly by licence. In these cases you are welcome to add these names after reading the banns in the manner of a simple notice. Then everyone in church can pray for all the couples together.

Secret summary

✓ **Make a priority of inviting couples to the reading of their banns.** They may not know they are invited.

✓ **You can also do this if you are the church where the couple lives.** The Weddings Project's banns invitation card also works for the home church.

✓ **Make sure you pray for the couple when you read their banns.** You can use the banns prayer from *Common Worship*.

✓ **Put the banns prayers in a good place in the service.** Not too early in case they miss them.

✓ **Make sure your church is geared up to look for the couple and say hello.** Ask for a photo from each couple as a focus for prayer. It might also jog your memory!

Moment Five:
The Big Day

The day dawns to the fifth moment that matters – the Wedding Day. It's a time for legal duty and holy celebration. Couples do want their wedding to be decent and dignified, but it should raise some smiles and maybe a few tears too. Churches may struggle to strike the balance between holy and happy, but it's the vicar who makes the difference on the big day.

- **Who should be in the driving seat when it comes to the service itself?**

- **What are the three things that elevate the big day experience above anything available anywhere else?**

- **How is it that the marrying priest can deliver all these at once, just by being themselves?**

- **How does the Church of England best welcome the wedding guests?**

- **How do we foster a spirit of collaboration with photographers and videographers who share the same space?**

———————

Two little words

Research teams for the Weddings Project interviewed couples marrying in Bradford and Oxford, surveyed brides at wedding shows and polled people in the general population. In this extensive and careful exploration they found two little words kept coming up time and time again. They are words which express the wonder of a church wedding. They are words that cause people who don't go to church to feel deeply compelled to choose it.

They may not be words that we would choose to describe our wedding day, but they are the words that sum up what the marrying generation means about theirs.

The first one sums up what only the Church can give: it's in the bones of the building and the timelessness of this ministry. It encompasses the gravity of the vows, the dignity and beauty of our sacred places, the value and respect accorded to the ordained, our ecclesiastical and legal customs and traditions. It may be something of an anticlimax, but the word that people today use to express all this is 'proper'.

But alongside 'proper' there is a desire for the wedding day to reflect something of the spirit of the marrying couple: their hobbies, their preferences, the people, places and things that matter to them and the life they have lived together. The word that people use for this essential element is 'special'.

This second idea is quite close to that of 'customisation'. It brings to mind trends that tend to make the news: biker weddings, underwater weddings, bi-plane weddings and horseback weddings are 'all the rage' according to recent news. One fashionable feature is for an owl to swoop down as part of the service with the rings in its beak and drop them onto a velvet cushion. This may have its genesis in Harry Potter books and films. In one West Country diocese we heard of an equestrian bride who rode to church on her favourite steed and who also wanted to invite it to the wedding. The vicar was happy to have the horse take its place behind the back row at the bottom of the bell tower.

The Weddings Project team found that this whole area has the capacity to bring some vicars out in a cold sweat. One told us: 'I prefer couples who aren't too imaginative. It's not about the day after all.' Another said: 'They see me as the expert and leave it to me.' And another agreed, adding hopefully: 'Different is not what they want.'

But many other vicars agreed with the opposite statement. They agreed that 'it's difficult to get people to understand how flexible the church is prepared to be'. This final opinion is one that gets many gestures of assent at Weddings Project events around the country.

So why should we make room for couples' own preferences and tastes in the way they design their wedding? Research for the Weddings Project found that it's more than just a matter of courtesy. To try to isolate the effect, researchers interviewed two groups of people: those that did not feel free to choose elements of the service which were distinctly personal to them, and those that felt very free to do this. Of those that did not feel free at all, only 4% were very interested in becoming more involved with the church after their wedding. But among those who felt very free to choose elements of the service that were distinctly personal to them – *on this measure alone* – 13% were very interested to get more involved with the church and the people there.

This is a finding that makes complete sense intuitively. If a couple feels that it's their wedding, they are more likely to feel it's their church. And if they feel it's their church, they are more likely to keep coming back. So there is a measurable church growth implication to saying yes to a couple's desire for their wedding to be 'special'.

In the mind of most couples there is no desire to increase the 'special' at the expense of the 'proper'. They want both, held in holy and human balance. The desire for 'proper' means it would be highly unlikely for them to want to remove reference to God from the service. The desire for 'special' might mean that a couple asks to embellish or rework their vows. Of course you can't lawfully agree to this, but you can give this creativity room in the service, as a song, a poem or a prayer.

But other things that are *special* for them might present as *improper* to us in church, and some brides sense that they ought not to ask the vicar for something special to them, lest they be considered vulgar in taste or temperament.

It was Thomas Jefferson who said: 'On matters of principle stand like a rock, on matters of taste swim with the current.' And research did discover some tension in churches over exactly what requires swimming and what standing. A few told us they agonised over where to draw the line.

One couple who wanted their dog at the wedding found their wish was one which the vicar favoured, but which the churchwarden did not. The dog lost. In other churches they've been welcoming dogs at weddings for years, and take seriously the idea that they can be as much part of the family as children. A vicar in Carlisle said to us: 'I have to work on the basis that if I say 'no', it's because I think Jesus would. I hardly ever say it.' When it comes to a couple's children in the service, the Church of England is widely sensitive and creative.

You'll know from previous chapters how difficult it can be for couples to admit to the vicar that they have children. So they receive it as grace if, in the context of the service, you simply recognise and respond to their children. Some brides – unsure about asking the vicar – have asked the Project team via the website if their toddler son can walk them down the aisle. We have heard how churches welcome the children to say the prayers, or to receive the blessing with mum and dad, or in the lighting of candles visually to express the newly formed family. The stories children tell about mum and dad can make charming vignettes or a fresh and funny sermon focus. All these things are inexpensive gifts for a church to give. But they are often expensively received by couples and their guests, as tender touches of God.

But if there *are* tensions in the crafting of the wedding day, the team asked the Archbishop of York: Who is in the driving seat? He had no doubt:

> 'If they want to be in the driving seat, it is *their* wedding – not *your* wedding. You are like a guest at the Holy Spirit's party – you're providing hospitality. You should let people feel relaxed. It's nothing like inviting people to come to your home and then you say: 'Now. This is my home and these are the rules and this is the way you are going to behave.' My friends, not many people will want to come to your home. You see, churches are places of hospitality.'

The importance of giving permission was reinforced by interviews we did with couples who did not get that message from their marrying church. A groom from Oxford Diocese, speaking to researchers on video about his big day, explained how the vicar took the view that the church 'would not be dictated to' about what went where in the service. The young man reflected on this with a sharp intake of breath as if to say 'OK, let's not go there'. You can probably guess how inclined he was to stick with church after the wedding.

A bride from Bradford had a similar experience: 'We'd come up with a couple of ideas about hymns and readings that we wanted, and we asked to have them "here and here"' (she gestured with her hands) '... you know, within reason, within what the vicar was suggesting. But she said "we always have the readings here and here and that is how we will have it. "' The quiet offence that is taken when a church lays down the law is palpable. But it is unlikely that the vicar will find out how these restrictions made couples feel. The fact of 'hypocrisy' will mean a bride or groom is easily persuaded to give in.

On the other hand, consider this analogy from a groom in the Oxford area. He described his wedding as excellent for this reason: 'From the start it was clear there was a director and there was a choreographer ... the bride was the director and the vicar was the choreographer.'

What does this look like when it happens? Researchers recorded an interview with Steve from Bradford whose parents died between his engagement and wedding. He and his new wife told the story of their vicar, Andrew, who took this central sadness as direction for the choreography of their wedding. Steve's wife said, 'the ushers gave each lady a carnation and it had a little note tied to it and it just said this was in memory of Steve's parents.' There was a point at which the guests held the flowers high and remembered Steve's mum and dad. A day of sadness because of loss, a day you wouldn't want to return to? Not at all.

'We've watched our wedding video trillions of times,' his new bride said. Steve thumped his chest, saying, 'I couldn't – hand on my heart – ask for anything better. On the day it's fantastic. The organist is winking at you – it's brilliant.'

And did those feet ...?

It is a hymn that is roguishly described as four questions with the answer 'no', and a small number of vicars don't like it at weddings. But it's a hit for this marrying generation, and was good enough for William and Kate at Westminster Abbey. It's the top choice by couples using the online ceremony planner at www.yourchurchwedding.org

'Jerusalem', being so well known, is lustily sung.

The Weddings Project researchers did interview a bride who was denied this choice of hymn. She explained on video how it felt to be told 'no'. 'We felt quite strongly that we really liked that hymn and at some point during the service we wanted to sing it. And the vicar felt it was inappropriate for a wedding. As to whether we'd looked into all the words ... well, we just felt strongly that we wanted that hymn. So that was a little debate going on, because she didn't want us to have it.'

For a little guidance on the spiritual propriety of this choice, the Weddings Project went to the Bishop of Wakefield, Stephen Platten, who chairs the Liturgical Commission. He said, 'I think "Jerusalem" is chosen because it's a very well-known hymn and it's almost a national hymn. But one of the great things about it is that it started off as a piece of poetry by William Blake talking about where he [Jesus] lived really, and why shouldn't that be picked up as one possibility when we're getting married? The context is hugely important, it's not just us, it's actually the place from which we come and all that we bring with us in terms of our own life experience. So I think people should be given plenty of freedom to choose those hymns that they think are going to work for them.'

Customisation and personalisation

The Weddings Project's research journey often felt like shining a light into a dark room – we didn't know what the beam would pick out next. And in this area something did emerge, fairly late in the process. It led us away from 'customisation' to a new idea: 'personalisation'.

One couple from Oxford gave the hint of it, in an interview with a researcher filmed in their living room. The newly wed bride said:

> 'I can very clearly remember her saying a few things, about how we'd met and where you'd proposed ... just a few things. Everybody was laughing I remember that. It was really nice because she had made it personal – I can imagine you would just go through the service, read it out, but she'd really taken time, it was really special.'

'Personal' is a word that emerges in wedding magazines like *You and Your Wedding*, which published the story of a great church wedding in the Diocese of Rochester. The Cape Town-born bride, marrying her Kentish sweetheart in his home village of Borstal, wrote:

> 'Personalisation was important for me because I needed that touch of Africa. As a surprise for me, our vicar, Esther, put an African cloth on our register table, which was so special.'

'Special' is the main word brides and grooms use to talk about the elements of the service that cause them to sigh delightedly inside. But who unlocks that door? Only the vicar who marries them. It's personal. Researcher Tamar explains:

> 'What we meant by customisation is couples being offered a range of options around hymns or decoration so that they could customise the service the way they always wanted it to be. Now in fact what emerged is that, if people are choosing a church wedding, in general they want something fairly traditional, so the range of options doesn't have to be that broad. But customisation is different from personalisation, which is making the ceremony something where they feel there's a human element the vicar introduces.'

'Bringing the human in' as Tamar tells it, happens in three main ways:

> 'One is when they have a sense that the vicar really knows them, and is able to talk about them as individuals, make a joke about them whatever it is. The second thing which really moved couples was when the vicar did something a bit off script – that revealed the vicar and their personality. So couples mentioned the bit when the vicar tied their hands together and how moving that was. And the third way of personalising is when the vicar does something to include the rest of the guests – to really help them feel part of it. And all these three things are what people remember. They bring the wedding above a slightly more transactional experience they may have elsewhere.'

We thought it was fascinating how Tamar, not an expert in the rituals and liturgies of the Church of England, picked out the moment when 'the vicar tied their hands together' as a personal moment between the priest and them. It may reveal that when couples experience what are quite familiar parts of the liturgy to us – like the moment when the stole is wrapped around their hands – they experience it as particularly fresh and meant for them. They really are seeing it for the first time!

You may remember the Maundy Thursday when the newly installed Archbishop of Canterbury washed feet in the cathedral and was commended by PR Week as breathtaking in his imagination and creativity. Sometimes the most ancient things are received as a great big gift to a culture that has never seen them before.

So here is the research case:

- If they get to know you
- If you get to know them – and can show this in the service
- If you include and involve the guests

then these three things will elevate the church wedding experience above anything available anywhere else.

And finally: jokes for sermons

In our tour of England we have been asked to refresh the clerical supply of wedding jokes. One vicar told us that his long experience of solemnising matrimony had worn out his joke book and he was no longer convinced of the truth of the saying 'the old ones are the best'. I suppose we have learned through all this research that jokes about marriage need now to give way to friendly personal anecdote. They do not have to be funny in the way Morecambe and Wise were funny. They do have to reveal something of your knowledge of the couple in ways that will make them and their guests laugh with a sense of fond recognition. One bride told our researchers how funny she found it when the vicar explained in the sermon that he shared her predilection for excellent coffee. It brought the house down. Now that's a joke you wouldn't find in a book.

Working with colleagues

When we asked vicars about some of the challenges of wedding ministry today, it wasn't long before they mentioned photographers. Photographers who move around too much, who disturb the sacred atmosphere, or who get a little too up close and personal. Some told us they sometimes feel they need to defend the couple against the photographer and so preserve the properness of their church wedding for them. Of course this sounds laudable, and sometimes it is.

The Weddings Project went to Durham diocese to ask the Bishop of Jarrow, Mark Bryant about this. In the light of his experience, what did he think the Church's approach to photographers should be? He said:

'I'm really quite unfazed by this. Photography is now the way we show that something is special. I've worked with couples over the years for whom life has been quite difficult, and their wedding is one day of their lives when they will have people photographing them. They'll be like Posh and Becks for just one day. And I think God can cope with that. And if God can cope with that it's probably up to me to try to cope with it as well.'

The Bishop suggested God would be most relaxed about photographers in heaven and he looked forward to a day when legions of them would dart around the throne of God vigorously snapping the Holy of Holies. And he added, 'It will be really important, a couple of weeks after the wedding, for the mother of the bride to be able to take the album into work.'

Capturing memory – memorialisation – is everywhere, and of course it's normal for the marrying generation to want to be able to look back on a pictorial record of the most important day of their lives.

We asked churches who didn't have photographer problems how they avoided them. These churches work at making friends with colleagues commissioned by the couple before the big day. Most commonly they do this by making good use of the rehearsal to meet the photographer to walk and talk things through. Others recommended particular photographers with whom they had a good rapport. Of course it's well worth thinking about this, as altercations just before or during the service can be heartbreakingly unforgettable.

So there are photographers, and then there are videographers.

I used to be a TV news producer, and so it was my business to drive around England with burly cameramen and all the associated gear to secure interviews for *News at Ten*. (Cameramen used to joke that they had to remember enough kit to fill a whole van while your average journalist just needed a pen, and would invariably forget that and need to borrow the cameraman's.)

It wasn't so very long ago that broadcast quality footage was only possible with hefty cameras, acres of cabling and banks of lights. And there's no doubt that until fairly recently the presence of a TV camera in church usually indicated that something highly unusual and faintly glamorous had hit town, such as *Songs of Praise*, or Disney or some other vast commercial endeavour.

But now if someone's filming a wedding, it's more likely to be someone like my Auntie Angela, who was just getting into videography on the day I was married. My wedding was mainly recorded from inside her handbag. But now even professional videographers can travel light. They can get close to their subject from quite far away because of powerful zooms. They can get a good picture even in low light conditions. And they don't need cables or to borrow your plugs – long battery life means they are now self-contained. The most they'll need from you is a feed from your PA system.

It's difficult to see how it costs a church anything at all to have a video camera in the building. Because of the advances in technology, it's just not so much of a big deal – practically – for a church to say yes to a couple's request to have their wedding filmed. But, more than that, there could be a marriage-care advantage to saying 'yes' to a couple who would like to have their wedding service filmed.

To check out this idea we went to meet newly wed Zoe, whose wedding was broadcast on Radio 4's *Sunday Worship* as part of their coverage of the changes that the Marriage Measure would bring. Zoe told us:

> 'When I hear something about a wedding, it makes me think I'm going to listen to my wedding again on my laptop, and when I do I always end up in tears.
>
> I think it's because life gets crowded and busy and you forget just how special it was. It's really lovely to be able to go back to a recording and remember.'

Of course, brides who watch their wedding video 'trillions of times' as one Bradford bride delightedly put it, see those vows they made over and over again, too.

We think a video of their vows might help them keep them. Welcoming a couple's desire to have their wedding filmed is to give them a gift that could protect their marriage for the long haul.

Two questions about organists

The Weddings team didn't expect to have a particular focus on organists, but in the short life of the Project two particular challenges from brides have come centre stage. The first is about what organists charge when a wedding is filmed. Here's one bride, Sarah, who's planning a wedding in Lancashire:

'What bothered us most is because we're having the wedding filmed we have to pay double the organist's fee … for some reason. And when we asked why, they said it was something to do with copyright … performing rights, or something like that. But we just thought, well is it their music to copyright? It's expensive as it is, so charging double is a bit much. And that was the first thing we talked about, me and my partner, when we got into the car after the meeting at church – where is this money going, and why do they have to do this?'

In order to get an answer to Sarah's question we went first to CCLI, the Church's copyright licensing authority. They confirmed that if you have a Church Copyright Licence (CCL) to let you copy hymn and song words on Sundays then you're covered for your weddings too – even if the wedding is recorded. Of course there are some technicalities. A few pieces of Christian music – one or two popular for weddings – aren't covered by the licence, but CCLI is keen to get them under their umbrella to make life easier for churches. For more about which they are, go to http://www.yourchurchwedding.org/hymns-media-player.aspx where you can see 30 wedding hymn favourites and all the copyright details.

This assumes that your Sunday congregation is the same size or bigger than your wedding congregations, so you are absolutely covered. Church music copyrighting has always allowed for housebound members hearing Sunday services later by means of a recording, and it's that longstanding facility that covers your wedding worship too, so no extra money is due to CCLI when a church holding a licence says yes to a couple who want to have their wedding filmed.

If you don't have a CCL or you usually have more guests at a wedding than come on a Sunday, you can get a temporary event licence instead. This offers a fortnight's cover and can be bought from CCLI as and when required. A professional videographer will know that if she is filming the whole wedding day, including the disco at the reception and then editing a film together of the whole day with music dubbed over, she will need to make her own arrangements for copyright cover. But all you need to know as a church is that you're covered if you have CCL cover, and you shouldn't feel under pressure to worry about anyone else's cover; the responsibility is theirs.

So what about music played on CD at a wedding or music played live? Well, the Performing Rights Society does not seek royalties from churches: they are exempt.

Our investigations took us to Salisbury and the headquarters of the Royal School of Church Music. The Director, Lindsay Gray, was attempting to undo a previously approved explanation from an RSCM spokesman who had suggested that playing for a wedding when a camera is filming puts 'extra pressure' on an organist. His idea that this requires compensation to the tune of 100% of the original fee was not going down well with vicars around the country.

So Take Two at the RSCM, and Lindsay Gray told us on video, 'I'm a real-ist: times have changed from the days when having a camera in church was something strange and unusual.' Sitting on an organ stool and holding up his iPhone to the camera, he said, 'Nowadays anyone can come along and take pictures on their mobile phone. So there is an argument for having a set fee for organ music whether the wedding is filmed or not.'

There is a well-established idea in the world of professional music, recorded in the context of a paid performance, that a musician should be paid more if more people will enjoy it later. But a wedding is not a ticketed event, and it will usually be most enjoyed again by the smallest number of people: the family and friends of the couple. This small group of people may regard the music as an incidental feature of the video. So 100% extra is a particular dif-ficulty for today's marrying public. You may not find out about this difficulty from the couples yourself: notice how Sarah said it was the first thing she and her partner talked about in the car on the way home. That's 'hypocrisy' at work. Whatever you ask of couples they will have this sense that you hold all the cards. They will try not to complain except privately to each other or to us at www.yourchurchwedding.org, out of fear that you will withdraw their church wedding from them.

Despite the RSCM Director's realism, their model contracts, available online, still justify an extra fee of 'up to 100%' if a wedding is filmed. But this issue is not going away.

Copyright and welcome

So copyright, and longstanding practices around recording a wedding, can sit in that uncomfortable gap between the 30-year-old bridal generation and the 62-year-old churchgoing one.

Most churches have taken the view that straining at gnats while swallowing camels is not what it's about, and attend to two main things which take the strain out of all this. First they buy an appropriate licence from CCLI which does the job on copyright for weddings too, at no extra cost.

Second, they work with their organist to frame an agreement that works, and write it down. The agreement should bear in mind the church's call to share in the welcoming and transforming mission of God. So it should be framed in the light of what couples think and feel if their organist double charges, or charges and does not play.

Some churches are still confused by these things, and that's understandable since different advice has come to them from different directions at different times. We would just ask any church to be clear, when they talk about copyright, that that is what they are talking about. Sometimes it is used as a 'catch all', to justify all manner of positions on filming and photography of public worship.

In one or two places we have been asked about the practice of charging copyright for the words of the liturgy. I'm very happy to confirm that the Archbishops' Council does not require payment for the reproduction of the words of services. A simple acknowledgement will do.

And if you are concerned with copyright payments due if videos are uploaded to social networking sites, please be assured. This is not an issue for you if you're not doing the uploading. It is in any case a huge headache for the whole wide world of copyright law, which cannot keep up with the pace of change and the free sharing of material. Jill and Kevin's wedding entrance dance, to the music of Chris Brown, has been viewed 70 million times, and Mr Brown didn't receive a cent (although legitimate sales of the track in question did consequently rise).

Some churches have 'contracts' which they ask the couples to sign guaranteeing they will not do this or that with the footage of the wedding. The validity of these sometimes unfriendly pieces of paper has not yet been tested in law.

The fear that the vicar will do something embarrassing is usually the root of this. Read on to the next chapter to see how unfounded that fear is.

The other question

I said there were two questions which brides ask. The other came to us from brides like Nicola from Sheffield. Nicola is a Christian businesswoman, who employs other young people in a smart and growing communications company in the city. Nicola is married to Pete, who is a professional concert musician and a worship leader for the biggest church in the area. So they are not only a Christian couple, they are a musical Christian couple. Nicola said:

> 'So, we had to go and see the vicar a few times before our wedding, and he explained to us that we would have to pay for the organist even though he or she wasn't going to be there. We questioned it, of course, but he said "well that's tradition and that's what we do in the church, so you're going to have to pay fifty pounds for the organist not to be there."'

Pete added:

> 'It didn't feel great to have to pay for someone not to play. And we were already going to quite a bit of expense for our own musicians to be there. My message to vicars would be there's no need to lay this extra charge on people. It's not very welcoming. So don't do it.'

Many organists are generous and laid back on these matters, and many recognise how brides and grooms may have a friend or family member who wants to play for them as a wedding present. They understand how that gift is undermined if they have to pay the resident organist nonetheless. One vicar at a Weddings Project event wrote in feedback under 'motivation to change current practice': 'I'm going to go home and hug my organist and tell her what a wonderful woman she is.'

These two issues are examples of flashpoints which can emerge when long-standing practices collide with the expectations of a new marrying generation. They have caught the attention of the Church of England nationally. One General Synod member asked the Archbishops' Council to 'get a grip' on what he called these 'antediluvian cartels'. These two things, at a time when the Church is trying to encourage more weddings, are perceived to be putting obstacles in people's way.

Of course, couples are under no obligation to have music at their wedding and if they don't choose music then, by law, you cannot ask them to pay for any. But if they do choose it, then it will trigger the church musician's contract or agreement, whatever that is.

The Weddings Project team asked the Bishop of Rochester, James Langstaff, about this, in the context of overall fees and charging for weddings. 'It is a difficult one,' he admitted. And the answer?

> 'Make sure you have an agreement with your organist, whether that's a contract with someone who's full time, or a working agreement with someone who's very part time, so you all know what you're doing. So if anyone comes along and says they don't understand this or that, you have something to fall back on. And again, I'd say about all of this, this is to do with the mission of the church. And we can't be condoning practices, whether it's an organist, a bell ringer, or anybody, which say that the church is greedy and money grabbing. That's not what it's about.'

Guests

By the time the big day comes round you've had the chance to be in touch with the couple for an average of 18 months. But their guests? Let's say that the window of opportunity with them is about one hour. So how well does the Church of England welcome guests at a wedding? The Weddings Project team went to 46 weddings in Bradford and Oxford one summer to find out.

It was hard not to feel like OFSTED during this experiment though we were keen to reassure the churches we visited that we just wanted to get the feeling of being a guest at a wedding in the church; that was all. The learning started before we even took our seats. Before the service even began, we noticed things about guests that might be true of guests where you are too.

The first is that they are so reluctant to enter the building. Guests congregate in the porch or chat just outside the door. Women shiver in off-the-shoulder finery, men kick the floor and look unsure. So why don't they come in, it's not difficult is it? Well, it might be more difficult than we think.

We wondered whether the sense of hypocrisy which research uncovered in the couples who came for a wedding could be just as evident in their guests. They don't go to church as a rule. Does that make them feel profoundly uncomfortable, standing there at the door? Might that come from a sense that they are 'not particularly religious' and in a place where religious people are found. Or is it more practical than that: do guests today just feel as if they don't know the drill: where to sit, whether to sit, where to put their children, if they should whisper, how to sing, when to stand, sit down again and so on? Whether it is hypocrisy in action or just the ordinary discomfort of unfamiliarity, the job of welcoming guests well is no simple thing.

Especially as we have fewer than 60 minutes to do it.

But watching from the sidelines at these weddings one summer, we found some simply brilliant things that vicars do at weddings to put guests at their ease, and they all begin in that golden time you have when everyone's assembled but *before the bride comes in*. No bride wants the theatre of her arrival crowned with housekeeping messages about mobile phones and confetti. So the great priestly task is to get all that over with beforehand. In so doing, you can put the guests at their ease before the bride starts the service proper.

We found the anxiety in the church reduced when the vicar drew everyone together with a smile, introducing themself by their first name. First off they set out the fact that the guests actually have a job to do. Male guests told the Weddings team during this exercise that they particularly appreciate the idea of something practical to do. It helps make them feel comfortable. So when the vicar explains that the job to be done is to make a promise today, to support and uphold this couple in the years to come, men do respond well to that. Practising that promise puts them at ease.

If you rehearse the promise before the bride comes in it helps everyone get used to hearing their voices raised in church. So the vicar explains how they'll make the promise in the service, and their cue will be the question:

'Will you, the family and friends of this couple, support and uphold them in the years to come?'

And the vicar says s/he's looking for the guests to raise the roof on the responding promise:

'We will!'

Now, as every pantomime artist knows, it always takes a couple of goes to get full audience participation. But at the moment the congregation is belting out the promise and smiling back at you you'll know you've done a lot in a little time. You have revealed to your guests that the church is not a library or a monument, rather it is a place that reverberates with joyful promise-making. You have made the men feel like they are not a spare part – they have a proper job to do. You have revealed yourself to be a warm likeable person with a first name and you have given permission to talk to you afterwards. And you've communicated to parents that their children may also raise their voices. All this is first-class missional input, and the bride's not even there yet.

And then, when it gets to the point in the service when the guests make their promise, they will give it with such gusto that the bride is surprised by the energy, volume and love in the room. You have instantly revealed to the couple that you have made a good connection with their guests, which – you will remember from earlier in this chapter – is the third critical element of a great church wedding.

In the Weddings team we found this liturgical lever such a magical relaxant for the anxious wedding guest that we made a card out of it. The guest card is on one side a record of the promise the guests will make that day, and on the other it is a prayer card so they can keep that promise with prayer all the days afterwards. We found that female guests particularly responded to the idea of praying for the couple to keep their promise, and a card to keep by the bed or at the office was a winning idea.

We trialled this card at these 46 weddings and made some changes to the wording, colours and functions. It flags a special part of the weddings website www.yourchurchwedding.org/guests where guests can find a great church near them after a wonderful wedding with you. It's one of our most popular resources in the Weddings Project range and it works as a gift from the church to the guests. It's a gift to hold in their hand as they rehearse their promise at the start of the service, and something to take away and a reminder for prayer. The closer the guests are to the couple the more likely it is to be taken away (but if any are left behind they can be used at a subsequent wedding.) Find out more at www.yourchurchwedding.org/project

Giving a gift seems to absolve the guests from that sense of hypocrisy they have when they first arrive (just as the welcome folder can melt a bride's heart when you first meet her). The important thing, we found, is intentionally to put it into their hands when they arrive (in the order of service, not just left in the pews). Guests need to know they have been given it as a gift and they are welcome to take it away. They won't naturally assume that it is theirs to keep.

One vicar told us that after she'd used these cards for the first time she had eight conversations of a deep or spiritual nature with guests at the reception (not a level she'd ever found with guests before). So there may indeed be something about giving a gift in the context of a friendly first-name-terms welcome which sets the scene for a good response from the guests.

Confetti and cash

As far as the giving out of the more mundane housekeeping notices goes, we made a few notes too. We found that the vicars who made the best impression on guests had worked to minimise the 'shalt not' element of the necessary notices. So for example one Bradford vicar made a point of saying: 'Don't forget to turn your mobile phone *back on* when the service ends.' We didn't hear many notices discouraging confetti, but when we did we observed a resulting nervousness in the guests striving to throw it in the places pointedly highlighted for 'safe throwing' (given, perhaps, how prone it is to drift). Most vicars seemed more keen to make the guests feel at home, even if it involved a little sweeping up later, and that included urging the children to stand on the pews or come to the front for a good view, encouraging congregational milling about during the register time, and restaging 'paparazzi moments' for anyone who'd missed a crucial close up in the service.

On the matter of asking for money from guests at weddings, you may know how comfortable it feels for you to ask. Some vicars may make an instinctive assessment of the congregation before quipping self-consciously about the roof. One vicar even said, 'I hate to ask this of you, but I'll get it in the neck from the treasurer if I don't.' Some wonder why the usual health warning issued before the collection plate on a Sunday (if you are new or just visiting please let it pass by) could yet apply to weddings. In the poorest parishes on our tour no collection was made and no plates were left out. One vicar in such a place said, 'We'd prefer our guests to feel like guests here.'

There is nothing at all unlawful about asking couples for a freewill offering after fees and charges have been agreed, and there's similarly nothing unlawful about asking their guests. But to find out how it felt to be asked, researchers interviewed couples whose guests were asked for money during the service, or who themselves were asked for a donation over and above what had been agreed in fees and charges. What emerged is that of those who were asked for more money, six out of ten said they were uncomfortable about it to a greater or lesser extent.

This does not mean that people won't pay. But it does mean more often than not there is a negative charge associated with the request. Together with all those dark stereotypes about churches only being interested in your money there are these facts about newcomers feeling hypocritical and nervous and ill at ease. You may decide that adding to this cocktail of discomfort is unkind, even if it advantages the roof. Some churches don't think a request for money brings in enough to compensate for the discomfort of asking for it and being asked. They often wisely deal with this tension by seeking the couple's preferences on the matter. Sometimes churches offer a collection for a charity of the couple's choice, which positions the church more positively and seems – some churches report – to be much more fruitful. However, we are just bringing you the news of what couples and guests really think of this practice. What you do with the news is for you to decide.

Secret summary

✓ **Consider afresh the visual symbols of the Church of England's liturgy.** Try to imagine you have never seen them before.

✓ **Think about the ways you have helped a couple express gratitude or remembrance in their marriage service.** Consider their response.

✓ **Look up the guidelines for incorporating baptism or thanksgiving for the birth of a child into a marriage service.** You can find these at www. yourchurchwedding.org/project. Think about offering this in the context of a wedding if you have never done so before.

✓ **Look at the three things a priest does which elevates the wedding day experience above anything available elsewhere.** Consider the extent to which your open and quick response at 'first contact' lays a foundation for a wonderful wedding day.

✓ **Welcoming a couple's request to film their wedding might one day save their marriage.** If the church where you are has a policy to discourage filming (or lay extra charges on a couple who want it), take time to review this.

✓ **Review your contract or agreement with your organist in the light of what couples think and feel about:**

  – double charging when a wedding is filmed;
  – paying an organist who doesn't play.

✓ **Use the time before the bride comes in to introduce yourself to the guests by your first name.** Keep housekeeping notices permissive and practise the promise the guests will make.

✓ **Consider cancelling collections at weddings** or seek the couple's preferences on the matter.

Moment Six:
The Warm Glow

By the time the wedding is over, a typical busy church has waved the couple off, prayed them God speed, and got on with the next busy thing. However, deep in the heart of the couple something has warmed towards the church, and it is mission critical to keep it glowing.

- **How well do we do weddings in the Church of England?**
- **Would you like to have marks out of ten for the way you do weddings?**
- **Would you like to know if there was something you could do to make them even better?**
- **And if you would like to know, would you prefer not to ask?**
- **How can you use this sixth moment, a month after the wedding, to be in touch with the couple again, just when they'd love to hear from you?**

How well we do weddings

One of the pervasive ideas in the Church of England is the faint suspicion that we – corporately at least – don't do weddings very well. And it's a morale sapper. If you ask vicars at the beginning of one of the Weddings Project presentations why church weddings are on a steeper slide than weddings in general, one of the answers you'll always get is that castles and hotels must do it better than the church from start to finish. Well, it stands to reason. Doesn't it?

To try to find the truth, the Project's researchers asked 822 people marrying in the Diocese of Bradford and in the Buckingham archdeaconry of Oxford. They were interested to speak to couples at three different points on their church wedding journey; before, during and after their wedding day. The **first** group were quizzed even before they were married, when they had just enquired about a wedding and received the welcome of the church. The **second** group were all freshly newly wed – they were mainly asked about the big day itself. And the **third** group had just reached their first anniversary. Through this final sample we wanted to assess the standard of care they received from their marrying church after the wedding.

It was a self-selecting survey mainly conducted by contacting couples from marriage register data and asking them if they would be willing to tell their stories. This group of 822 were those who came forward from a wider sample of 2,800. Their answers were recorded graphically and some of the respondents went on to be interviewed in more depth and on video.

Remember, all these couples are speaking to secular researchers, not people wearing dog collars lest that skew the responses one way or the other. This research team was more used to finding out public responses to fizzy drinks, training shoes and manifesto promises. So what did they find out about what the marrying public thought of the Church of England's weddings ministry?

In the **first** group of people, not married yet but welcomed to church for a wedding, nine out of ten of them rated their experience of church as good, very good or excellent. They were asked to choose words that applied to the way they rated the church in the practical preparations for the wedding. Overwhelmingly this group chose words like *reassuring, approachable, professional* and *inspiring* over *off-putting, intimidating, disorganised* and *dull*. So nine out of ten couples are happy with their church wedding experience even before the wedding. It's the sort of review rating which, if you were in another line of work, might herald big bonuses and perks.

You will get your reward of course (just not here).

The **second** group of people told a different story, and it came through loud and clear. Ten out of ten couples, just married in the Church of England in Bradford and Oxford, rated their experience as good, very good or excellent, and practically all of them would recommend a wedding at their marrying church to a friend. Even allowing for a streak of rose-tintedness about their wedding, these responses were outstanding. Couples in this group were asked to assess their vicar's contribution on and around the wedding day. Asked: 'did you find the vicar's words, prayers and sermon appropriate?' 97% agreed very much that they did. In fact no one had a bad word to say about the vicar on the day.

Then researchers compared the first and second groups to see if and how impressions of the vicar changed between booking the wedding and the day itself. What they found is that people thought their vicar more professional and in particular more inspiring the closer to the wedding they got. Comparing results from the group of new entrants with the group of newly weds, there was a notable leap in the percentage who rated the vicar as professional and inspiring. In particular, the number of people who thought their vicar was inspiring had doubled – from 44% to 88% between the opening stages of the church wedding journey and the wedding itself.

These findings were painting a picture of an on-the-day experience at least on a par with any other wedding venue (whose customer satisfaction scores are not usually published). We were also finding that what we offer on the day – our liturgy and the reassurance and guidance of the priest – were greatly and widely appreciated. Indeed our researchers were dazzled by the strength of these responses and the gratitude, positivity and regard shining through from the public in these two very different geographical areas of the Church of England. Where respondents had a negative experience, these were a very small part of the whole story.

So evidence shows that most people who persist with the idea of a church wedding, and who are not ultimately put off by ideas of their own hypocrisy or anything else, are greatly rewarded.

Aftercare: the bad news

So much for what the Church does which *can* be compared to castles and hotels – taking care of couples up to and including their wedding day. But how well does the Church do *after* the big day? Researchers found out by asking the first-anniversary group to assess their experience of their church in the year after their wedding day.

Only one out of ten of these couples, married for one year, rated this experience as excellent. The graphs tell a stark story here. Asked: 'Has the church where you got married kept in touch with you in any way?', most answered in the negative, in marked contrast to the satisfaction scores from the groups comprising new entrants and newly weds. In the anniversary group 53% just said no, the church did not keep in touch with them in any way. Another 34% said their marrying church 'kept in touch to a small extent'. Our researchers wondered if that was vicarious contact, so for example if the church is in touch with their parents and they are in touch with their parents, consequently the couples might *feel* a little bit in touch with the church. Only one in ten couples said yes, the church where they married kept in touch with them to a real extent in the year after their wedding.

But this is just of academic interest, isn't it, if the couples do not want further contact with the church after the wedding? If our newly weds actually want us to leave them alone after the wedding, then being in touch again would be at least a bit pushy. So our researchers quizzed the first anniversary couples more particularly: 'Would you have liked more contact from the church where you got married, less contact, or about the same?' And they told us straight: only one in a hundred sought *less* contact from their marrying church.

That's like saying, after you've bought a book online or theatre tickets or a coat, that you do not want the organisation you bought it from to send you news of subsequent special offers. I don't know if you're the kind of person who ticks the box that closes down further contact, but only one in a hundred couples would do that to their church after their wedding. That's so insignificant a number that statisticians would generally disregard it.

Meanwhile, what proportion is asking for more? According to our research 28% – that's almost 1 in 3 – said they actually wanted *more* contact from the church after the wedding. If we apply that figure to the number of weddings we do in the Church of England, that's more than 30,000 people actively open to sustained contact having experienced the ministry of the Church of England for their wedding. So in mission terms it's like this: after the wedding there is still at least an open door to us. Only one in a hundred would feel harassed or offended if the church was in touch again. And the potential is this: if we did keep in touch with only the people that wanted to hear from us, the Church of England could add to its number the equivalent of an extra diocese every year.

The warm glow

So much for low morale. When it comes to a wedding we have good reason to say in the Church of England that nobody does it better. In fact, our research experts advised that, because of the high quality of welcome, care and diligence we put into weddings, something like a 'warm glow' surrounds couples immediately after the event. This is not to be confused with wedded bliss; it is church specific. It's a warm glow about the vicar, the people in the church and the love they feel from them. Brides spoke to us about feeling enveloped in that love, feeling part of the family, and then feeling confused and a little bereft when it ended. This bride was filmed reaching out her arms in a gesture of embrace when she spoke about the warm glow her marrying church had left her with:

> 'It was such a special day for us, you kind of almost feel part of that family in a way and much closer to the church. So you've shared a very personal time, a very special day with that person, and then the relationship stops. It would be good to get something from the vicar who you've had that relationship with.'

Now, you might be feeling the slight chill of uncharity at this. After all this couple, by the time that they are married, clearly knows who their vicar is, where the church is, how to get there, and where the door is. So, if they feel so bereft because we don't get in touch with them, why don't they come all by themselves? What are they waiting for, a personal invitation?

Well yes, actually, they are – just because of the fact of a couple's sense of hypocrisy, and their retreat into it after the wedding.

Consider how they feel. They came to you, they darkened your door and dared to ask you for a church wedding. You said yes, and now you have – in the couple's mind – delivered on that transaction. Why wouldn't they return to their original sense of hypocrisy and not believe it is permissible to knock on the door again?

And if that's the problem, what's the solution? One bride from Buckinghamshire put it this way:

> '... whether it's a little card or notelet or whatever it is, but just something to say we enjoyed your day or hope you enjoyed your day, it would be nice if you get the opportunity to come to church. No pressure, it's just something to follow up, because it's not the end of it. It shouldn't be the end of it.'

Sending a card was, our researchers said, the 'quickest win' for us in the Church if we believe, as many couples do, 'that it shouldn't be the end of it'. If all the work that went into establishing a connection is not sustained by the Church after the wedding, then this warm glow, which is rich in mission potential, is extinguished. And it does have to be the Church that makes contact again because of the fact of a couple's retreat into hypocrisy once the wedding day is over. If you're the sort of vicar who is used to getting cards from couples to thank you for a wonderful wedding, or postcards from their honeymoon, and if you put them on the mantelpiece and think 'oh well that's really nice of them ...' then think again. They might be trying to keep in touch with you.

If you're already a participant in the Weddings Project you'll probably be using the Weddings Congratulations card to send on the couple's wedding day. It's meant to land on their doormat in time for their return from honeymoon, and you're supported in sending it by a secure web-based diary system which reminds you in good time to send it. The card is designed to go from the home church and from the marrying church if they are different. We designed and wrote the Weddings Congratulations card to communicate gentleness and invitation. We did not need to go so far as to enclose a copy of the Bridge Diagram or an explanation of the Trinity. The key things it says are along the lines of what one couple told our researchers:

> 'Even if it wasn't very personal – we know summer's a really popular time – but maybe if the church made a card and your vicar just signed it and it said "hope you had a great wedding. Love from the church and then ... Andrew."'

This couple made the point, as did many brides, that even though the wider church family is in view by the time of their wedding, it is still the vicar – Andrew in this case – who is central to their focus and he or she remains the person who makes the most difference to them. That's why we say on the matter of sending of cards, that it doesn't matter who gets the reminder email, lines up the card, puts a stamp on the envelope and posts it. But please, for the sake of the growth of the Church of England, can you ensure that the vicar signs it?

A card is simple to send, and so are emails and other electronic means of communication. Keeping the warm glow alive no longer requires an hour's home visit with traffic jams, pay-and-display parking and tea and biscuits. In these days of texting and tweeting, a little thoughtfulness goes a long way. All these things help keep the warm glow alive. Whatever you do to sustain contact with your couple after their wedding, we estimate that the first 30 days are the richest territory for being in touch. The longer you leave it, the harder it gets to keep connected, as Tamar Kasriel explains:

> 'There is a warm glow following a church wedding, when couples have had a fabulous time, and they are very grateful to the church, to the vicar, but the half life of that warm glow is extremely short.'

When it does work, it sound like this. This Bradford newly wed is now mum to baby Alex:

'We just thought it would be a formality and that we'd be married but we've had a couple of emails from him, and he's been to the house. We see him in the supermarket and he always remembers your name. And he must do loads of weddings. And now we've got Alex, when he's a bit older we'll probably go back, now we've got him, take him to Sunday School.'

OK, this couple is in the 50% who can bump into their marrying priest in their local supermarket. The fact of social mobility and the Marriage Measure means the other half of the couples we marry will be in some other supermarket in some other parish after their wedding. But however you do post-wedding care, through an effective referral to the home priest, through a friendly text or email after the day, or sending a card, your couple will be warmed by the knowledge that you are still caring and praying for them, even though the wedding day is over.

How are you? How were we?

Early in the Weddings Project's work, many vicars were keen to find some way of getting more constructive feedback about how they do weddings. Many routinely receive thank-you cards for their weddings ministry, and greatly value these. But there was this nagging thought expressed to us: if you really had a development point about a wedding – and the vicar could really do with knowing it – would a thank you card be the appropriate vehicle? Not really.

On the other hand, how can the vicar really ask for robust feedback, since the fact of their asking might affect the response. 'We'd like to know how we're doing,' many told us, 'but we don't want to be seen to ask.' Others articulated the view that actual measurable post-wedding scores for the vicar would help on all sorts of levels: generally raising your game, being sure you're on the right track, marketing weddings in the parish. One summed it up beautifully, we thought: 'In our church we'd like to be known as investors in weddings.' There's no doubt that when vicars up and down England saw 'nine out of ten' and 'ten out of ten' scores from couples marrying in Bradford and Oxford they were even more keen to know what marks *they* would get for weddings they had done too. But of course there are people who'd rather not know, and find the whole marks-out-of-ten principle rather vulgar. 'Eugh', said one vicar frankly, of asking couples to rate their church wedding experience. 'It makes it feel like having your car serviced at the garage.'

Because of the fact of the warm glow and its tragically short half life, because of the fact that vicars are busy and because today's marrying generation is used to filling in online feedback about everything these days, the Weddings Project went to work. So if you're registered on the Weddings Project diary (the one that sends you reminders about when to send cards), exactly 30 days after their wedding your couple will get an automated email to fill in an online form at www.yourchurchwedding.org. Ten simple questions, and when they click 'submit', it lands in your inbox. Feedback is anonymous (though you might be able to work out who it is, arriving as it does a month after the wedding). The crucial thing is that it appears that the vicar is not asking but the website is. That's why it works so well, and vicars who use this function are tickled pink with the scores they get.

The incidental benefit of all this is that without you having to remember to do it, the couple will receive this 'how are you' message automatically. It expresses delight at being able to share in their wedding and asks them to explain a little more about how that experience was for them. So you'll be sending something in the 'warm glow' period and hearing back from your couple, without any extra input from you at all. Maybe what you get back will make you want to keep talking. We hope so. After all, as the brides say, the wedding *shouldn't* be the end of it, should it?

Secret summary

✓ **There's a warm glow about a church wedding, but its half life is extremely short.** Re-establish contact with a couple you have married in the 30 days after the wedding to keep that warm glow alive.

✓ **By now the whole church family has come into view but, in the mind of the couple, the vicar is still the primary focus of the relationship.** Think about a plan to graft these two new people into the life of the church.

Use events in the church's calendar to keep couples connected with their church.

✓ **This couple may live far away.** Make it part of your plan to alert the vicar in their home parish, and recommend them to him or her.

✓ **Have you ever got a thank you card and thought, 'oh that's nice' and done no more?** Consider that in sending it a couple might be trying to keep their friendship with you alive.

Moment Seven: First Anniversary

One year on, and most newly weds will take time to remember their wedding and all that's happened since. By this seventh and final moment, a church has been in touch with each couple for two and a half years; eighteen months before the day and a year after it.

- **Will you remember the anniversary of their big day?**

- **Why is this such a magic moment for a special invitation to church?**

———————

One vicar told the story of what happened when she made a little change to her weddings practice at this final anniversary moment. She left the Weddings Project presentation in Ely Diocese saying to herself, 'I could do this. I could send a card to the people I've married when their anniversary comes around.' When she was in touch with one couple the groom phoned to explain, with heartbreak in his voice, how his new wife and he were no longer together.

This momentary reconnection laid a path back to church for this young man, whose marrying priest became his counsellor. Chances are he might never have knocked on the door of the church again if the church had not knocked on his. It's a very unusual thing for a first anniversary to work out this way, although of course it may happen.

For most couples it's a happy moment to stop and remember. It's a table for two moment. It's a champagne and photo album moment. And it's an obvious moment for an invitation to church.

Why?

More than eight out of ten church weddings are on a Saturday. So, allowing for the occasional leap year, most first anniversaries are on a Sunday, presenting a chance to invite a couple back to church to experience the prayers and love of the church where they married – or the one close to home.

The Weddings Project created a first anniversary card to do just this, backed up with the reminder system so the vicar gets a nudge in enough time to sign and send it. It's in stock in 33 dioceses, and the team has begun to discover how churches love it. It's an easy and non-threatening way to get in touch with a couple. It invites them to church at a moment relating to their celebrations rather than ours. It's proactive. It's pastoral. And it's personal, if the marrying priest signs the card to communicate the best wishes of the whole church.

It's an idea we borrowed from the late Canon Eric Saxon of St Ann's church in the city centre of Manchester. His obituary, in the broadsheets, noted how he faithfully wrote to every couple he had ever married on each anniversary of their wedding. But we found the same practice alive and well in Worcester Diocese. One vicar, who has made this a ministry priority, reported that it doesn't take too much time and had some extraordinary results. After ten years of faithfully sending greetings to one particular couple on their anniversary, they turned up at church to see him. They were experiencing some difficulty in their marriage and they needed his help. Now, he says, this couple are deeply involved in church life and one is training for ordination.

Seven moments on the road

We have travelled a long way in a short time. On average, two and a half years separates the first contact moment and the first anniversary. That's about a thousand days. Not every couple will take 18 months to get to their wedding day – some engagements are longer, some shorter, but in most cases a couple is 'on our books' for two and a half years.

One thousand days. And out of those, there are *only seven moments* when the marrying priest needs to be in the lead if growing the church is what we want to do. Of course, that might mean growing someone else's church through actively referring your couple on to their home vicar. But the Weddings Project can help with that if you'd like us to.

This book turns 'doing weddings' into a road stretching from first contact until first anniversary. But it's frontloaded. As one Portsmouth vicar said to us on our national tour: 'First impressions count.' Getting the first moments right clears the way for a priest-to-couple connection that can extend after the day. All the evidence suggests that quickly introducing a couple to their marrying priest takes their seriousness seriously and gets you off to a flying start. The vicar becomes friend and evangelist to these two, who only plan to pass this way once.

One in four

How many couples say they actively seek more contact from their marrying church after their wedding? More than one in four, 28%.

How many couples say their Christian faith has increased through the experience of their wedding? One in four, 25%.

For how many couples has their wedding experience made them want to get more involved in church? One in four, 26%.

These findings are baseline figures, drawn from research in Bradford and Oxford before the resources and learning of the Weddings Project were made known. But whatever difference the Weddings Project has made through its system, it has this evidence to offer you, system free. For every four weddings you do, one couple is interested enough to stick with you. They may actually stick at their home church because that's closer to them. But they are open to the church, even after their wedding.

Secret summary

✓ **Invite a couple to church on or around their first anniversary.** Use the Weddings Project's online reminder system so you don't forget to send a card. Find out more at www.yourchurchwedding.org/project

✓ **If you are the home church, you can send this too.** The card is designed to come from both the home and marrying churches.

✓ **Consider how many weddings happen in the church where you are each year.** How would it affect your Sunday attendance if one in four couples did what they were minded to do, and stuck with their church after the wedding and grew in their faith and Christian commitment?

✓ **Think about the fact that, by attending to this book's findings, you might contribute to the growth of a couple's home church and not your own.** Does that bother you?

Afterword

That which was from the beginning, which we have heard, which we have seen with our eyes, which we have looked at and our hands have touched – this we proclaim concerning the Word of life.

1 John 1

I said at the beginning of this book that the Archbishops' Council wanted to see a difference, and they wanted the evidence to prove it. So what difference has the Weddings Project made?

The Council wanted to **attract more church weddings** in two trial areas, the Diocese of Bradford and the Archdeaconry of Buckingham in Oxford. The target was 5% more church weddings in each.

After two years of research and development, participating churches reported that their wedding bookings had increased by 10% (the Oxford pilot) and 50% (the Bradford pilot). Nationally, by 2010, all Church of England weddings were up by 4%.

A subsequent online survey of 125 participating clergy in Norwich, Ripon and Leeds indicated that as many as 43% had seen a rise in wedding bookings since hearing the research and using the Project's system. Follow-up after the wedding was as high as 68%. Only one vicar reported that participating in the Project had made his or her life more difficult.

The Archbishops' Council also wanted to **improve the popular perception of the Church of England's enthusiasm for marriage.** When the team first measured this, 67% of the population believed that the Church believed in marriage. A number of fresh undertakings in 2008 had a big effect: the launch of the Marriage Measure, the new website www.yourchurchwedding. org, a range of stories intentionally placed in the media, and national church support for wedding shows. After this concentrated effort, 74% were sure of the Church's enthusiasm, that's 4.2 million extra people who had been convinced.

On the third and most crucial aim, that of **improving stickability**, the weddings team had to find the key indicators which would drive this up. Before the Weddings Project did its work, no one knew for sure what these were. But if we had to write a 'stickability strategy' now it would have three things in it and here's what they would be:

1. Make sure the marrying priest is the **mainstay** of the couple's connection with the church. The vicar makes the difference, so the deliberate and quick assignment of a couple to their marrying priest really matters. If you delegate this work or if you delay, you cement a couple in their sense of unworthiness, and you will find it hard to retain them into the worshipping life of the congregation.

2. Welcome a couple's desire to make their wedding **personal** to them. That means responding through simple visual symbol to a couple's story. It's done through welcoming their guests and putting them at their ease. And it's by showing, in the context of the big day, that you are knowable and that you know and love this couple.

3. The third stickability driver is intentional follow up. This should begin quickly after the wedding day, since the warm glow that follows a church wedding fades quickly. Sustaining contact through the system offered by the Weddings Project will help. But for many churches just knowing that the couples would welcome further contact is enough to change longstanding practices.

So these green shoots are signs of the difference the Weddings Project has already made. When the team was ready to 'roll out' nationwide with its story and system of resources, the Archbishops' Council asked them to reach 5 dioceses in two years. In the event the team covered 33 dioceses in 14 months, working only where it was invited by the bishop and senior team in each place.

You can read the responses to that training at www.yourchurchwedding.org/project, but here's just one example from the Diocese of Derby:

'Brilliant! All the information was based on 'out there' research rather than what we think is going on. Felt that much of what you laid before us was transferable into other areas of ministry.'

In response to the call to apply the method, the Archbishops' Council has agreed to fund two new projects over the next five years. These will focus on the welcome the Church of England offers following the birth of a child and on its ministry to the bereaved.

Acknowledgements

Special thanks to the team:

John Barton, Paul Bayes, Jenny Cotton, Kate Bottley, Nick Devenish, Ruth Green, Sarah Kay, Aidan Platten and Denise Poole

Alexander McGregor at the Legal Office of the Archbishops' Council
David Churchyard at Christian Copyright Licensing International

Acknowledgement is due to the Archbishops' Council for all references to the Common Worship marriage service.

Index